HONORING THE ELDERLY

A Christian's Duty to Aging Parents

Rev. Brian L. De Jong

ISBN: 1548220353
ISBN 13: 9781548220358

DEDICATION

To my dear wife DeLou, to my six beloved children –
Samantha, Ian, Grace, Elijah, Cameron and Christian
and to their spouses and future spouses.

TABLE OF CONTENTS

ACKNOWLEDGMENTS

This book began as an adult Sunday School class at Grace Orthodox Presbyterian Church in Sheboygan, Wisconsin. Knowing that many families within our congregation grappled with the challenges of caring for elderly parents, I determined to put together a series of lessons on pertinent topics. The class featured lively interaction with many of the members sharing insights, experiences and challenges. My own contributions were of a Biblical and theological nature, and the class was an enjoyable experience. Several in the class felt the material was worth further development, and they encouraged me to put my notes into written form for publication. Special thanks goes to Bob and Debbie Boss and Lynn and Sandy Baatz for their contributions on the chapter on coping with dementia. I also greatly appreciate the encouragement from the Session and congregation at Grace OPC to keep working toward publication. My brother Greg and my cousin Ren were extremely helpful in fine tuning the chapter on financial issues. My wife has been another source of help and encouragement, especially in regard to numerous letters of rejection from prospective publishers. My parents also provided significant support by allowing us to come for summer writing retreats. But most of all, I am grateful to my Lord and Savior, Jesus Christ. Without the living and enduring Word of

God, there would be no wisdom on this or any other topic. By the Spirit's aid, this book has come to completion. May it bless many, and bring glory to the Triune God!

PREFACE

I t is no great secret that life is changing in the United States for the elderly and their families. The Centers for Disease Control reports that "life expectancy in the United States continues a long-term upward trend."(Health, United States, 2006 with Chartbook on Trends in the Health of Americans, Executive Summary, p.21.)   In their annual assessment entitled Health, United States, 2006 they state that "In 2004, life expectancy at birth for the total population reached a record high of 77.9 years (preliminary data), up from 75.4 years in 1990. Between 1990 and 2004, life expectancy at birth increased 3.4 years for males and 1.6 years for females (preliminary data)."

These changes are ascribed, in part, to advances in medical science and health care. The CDC reviews these developments in their report: "Over the past century, many diseases have been controlled or their morbidity and mortality substantially reduced. Notable achievements in public health have included the control of infectious diseases such as typhoid and cholera through decontamination of water; implementation of widespread vaccination programs to contain polio, diphtheria, pertussis, and measles; fluoridation of water to drastically reduce the prevalence of dental caries; and improvements in motor vehicle safety through vehicle redesign and efforts to increase usage of seatbelts and motorcycle helmets." (Health, US, 2006, p.21)

The news has not been entirely positive, though. The CDC acknowledges that "With longer life expectancy, however, comes increasing prevalence of chronic diseases and conditions that are associated with aging." (Health, US, 2006, p.21) Moreover, seniors are discovering that due to increasing medical costs, decreasing benefits from insurance and government programs (Social Security, Medicare and Medicaid), and the high cost of long-term nursing home care, they can outlive their retirement resources. Privately run nursing homes and care facilities face this same dilemma, and are forced to find creative solutions to help their residents.

These social, medical and cultural trends also impact the church and her members. The government statistics reflect the experiences of a growing number of Christian people. In a congregation with roughly one hundred members, we have sixteen families who have recently, or are currently caring for elderly parents. In most of these situations, serious health issues exist. Each of those families bears a burden. And realistically, there are no simple, easy, one-size-fits-all answers for the challenges they face.

Because we believe that the care of widows constitutes an essential component of "true religion" (James 1:27; cf. Deuteronomy 10:12-21), Christians simply cannot turn a blind eye toward the elderly in our midst. Honoring father and mother is foundational to godly living in a fallen world. The fifth commandment is a lodestar for Christian people wanting to respond in a Christ-like fashion.

In this study, I intend to consider the Biblical perspective on the care of the elderly, and to work through a variety of applications of the fifth commandment to these increasingly common scenarios. I seek to answer the question, "As a Christian, how should I take care of my aging parent?" The principles apply equally to any elderly person – whether a relative, a friend or simply a fellow Christian.

CHAPTER 1

THE BREVITY AND
DIFFICULTY OF LIFE

Birth, the first day of school, graduation, marriage, first job, first child, last child, twenty fifth anniversary, fiftieth anniversary, death – these are the mile markers of life. Whether it is "sweet 16", 21, 40, 50 or 65, our birthdays are all significant in their own way – each testifying that life is passing along.

Though our culture demands we live in a never-ending present, we are forced to admit sooner or later that our lives are short and difficult. The brevity and the difficulty of life are undeniable truths to people who refuse to shut their eyes to reality. Just yesterday we enjoyed the carefree days of childhood. Before we knew it we were launched into the adult world, speeding through our twenties and thirties. The older we grow, the faster time appears to accelerate. Already we have children, and then grandchildren. The corresponding decline of strength and stamina daily tell us that summer is over and autumn comes on apace. The winter of life cannot be far away.

Scripture explains what our experience indicates about the brevity and difficulty of life. There are many plain expressions of these facts in the Bible. Consider Psalm 103:15-16: "As for man, his days are like grass; As a flower of the field, so he flourishes. [16] When the wind has passed over it, it is no more, And its place acknowledges it no longer." This is not a proposition posed for debate, but a truism beyond dispute.

David spoke well when he said in Psalm 39:4-5, "LORD, make me to know my end and what is the extent of my days; Let me know how transient I am. "Behold, You have made my days *as* hand-breadths, And my lifetime as nothing in Your sight; Surely every man at his best is a mere breath. " Recognizing that man is "a mere breath" at best, David prayed that God would open his eyes to his own transience. David refused to delude himself, but longed to know the extent of his days and his own end.

Job testifies of the same reality. In Job 14:1-2 he says, "Man, who is born of woman, is short-lived and full of turmoil. Like a flower he comes forth and withers. He also flees like a shadow and does not remain."

The prophet Isaiah records a comparable observation in Isaiah 40:6-8 "A voice says, 'Call out.' Then he answered, 'What shall I call out?' All flesh is grass, and all its loveliness is like the flower of the field. The grass withers, the flower fades, when the breath of the LORD blows upon it; Surely the people are grass. The grass withers, the flower fades, but the word of our God stands forever."

The author of Ecclesiastes returns to this theme frequently. He advises his audience in Ecclesiastes 9:9 to "Enjoy life with the woman whom you love all the days of your fleeting life which He has given to you under the sun; for this is your reward in life and in your toil in which you have labored under the sun." (cf. 6:12; 11:10)

Rather than proclaiming the essential meaninglessness of life, the Preacher forces his readers to face the brevity of this life. (See Daniel Fredericks, <u>Coping with Transience: Ecclesiastes on the Brevity of Life</u> and <u>Ecclesiastes & the Song of Songs, Apollos Old Testament Commentary 16</u>, Downers Grove, Illinois IVP 2010.)

From this awareness, he gives counsel on how to cope with difficulty in the present and how to prepare for the future.

New Testament writers share this perspective. James counsels his readers along these lines when he says in James 4:13-14 "Come now, you who say, 'Today or tomorrow we will go to such and such a city, and spend a year there and engage in business and make a profit.' Yet you do not know what your life will be like tomorrow. You are *just* a vapor that appears for a little while and then vanishes away." Peter agrees in his first epistle, saying, "All flesh is as grass, and all the glory of man as the flower of the grass, The grass withers, and its flower falls away, but the word of the Lord endures forever."

Of all the wise men ever moved by the Holy Spirit to write on this theme, none excels Moses, the man of God. His prayer, as recorded in Psalm 90, touches this topic in a most searching way. He begins in vv.1-2 by reflecting on the eternality of God – "From everlasting to everlasting, You are God."

Moses next ponders death as God turns man back to dust: "⁴ For a thousand years in Your sight Are like yesterday when it passes by, Or *as* a watch in the night. ⁵ You have swept them away like a flood, they fall asleep; In the morning they are like grass which sprouts anew. ⁶ In the morning it flourishes and sprouts anew; Toward evening it fades and withers away."

What is to account for the brevity of life? Sure Moses identifies the source of the situation when he describes God's wrath against man's sin. Because our secret sins are illuminated in God's presence, we finish our years like a sigh. After a mere 70 or 80 lamentable years, we fly away.

All of Moses' reflections come to their climax in v.12, where he asks God to "teach us to number our days, that we may present to You a heart of wisdom." Life is short, hard and full of vexations. Soon it is gone and our spirits fly to God even as our bodies rest in the grave, awaiting that great and final day.

3

Reflecting on the brevity and difficulty of life can produce anxiety, frustration and despair. At points, the author of Ecclesiastes professed to hate life, and the fruit of all his laborious toil. Yielding to discouragement, he turned his heart over to despair. Perhaps you have known embittered seniors, who seem angry at the world because their best days are past. Older people who have soured on life can be deeply unattractive.

But this is not the only possible response to the brevity and difficulty of life. For a believer in Christ, these insights can contribute to the mature wisdom of old age. Yes, life is short and hard. Those are the predictable results of man's fall! God's wrath and curse justly abides on the creation – a fact shown by 'ravages of age' and the inevitability of the grave.

Viewed in a different light, these insights can help us in several different ways. First, the brevity of life reminds us to keep our priorities. If you believe that you have endless time on your hands, it is easy to pursue interests that are essentially trivial and eternally insignificant. Take the game of golf, for instance. While having a good short iron game would be crucial for a PGA pro on the tour, is it really so important for a forty-five year old businessman with a wife and four children? As any golfer will tell you, golf is a game that demands practice and precision. Gripping the club incorrectly, swinging it improperly, hesitating at the wrong point in the motion – they can all contribute to a shanked shot. To hone a very specialized aspect of golf will take many hours on the driving range – perhaps with an instructor giving lessons. Then you must use that skill in your game by playing on a regular basis – perhaps three or more times per week. If each round takes a minimum of three hours start-to-finish, you may need to dedicate 40 hours per month to perfecting your short iron game.

There are 720 hours in a month. You are asleep for 240 of those hours and at work for perhaps another 200 hours. In addition, you spend time eating, driving, shopping, attending church, watching TV, doing yard work and visiting with friends. Your free time dwindles due to natural limitations and the requirements of your life – do you really have 40 hours per month left for practicing your chip shot? Is that skill important enough to cause you to neglect your wife and ignore your children?

A realization of the incredible shortness of human life forces us to look long and hard at how we spend our time, energy, and resources. I have only limited time in an all-too-short life – is mastering my eight iron a higher priority than discipling my teenage son?

Thus our experience confirms what Scripture repeatedly teaches about the brevity and difficulty of life. Understanding this point can be a source of sorrow or it can be a component of godly wisdom. It can drive a man to despair or can guide him to live his days to the glory and praise of the God who made us frail children of dust.

Questions for Discussion

- From the preface, what changes increasingly face the elderly and their families? Have you seen evidence of this among those around you?
- What are the "mile markers of life?" What truth do they remind us about?
- How does our culture respond to the passing of life? Can you give examples?
- What does David realize in Psalm 39:4-5? What is his prayer?
- What agricultural comparisons are made by Job, Isaiah and Peter? How does this illustrate the brevity of human life?
- To what does Moses ascribe the difficulty of life?
- What is James' exhortation to his readers?
- What are possible responses to the brevity and difficulty of life?
- What limitations impact our priorities?

CHAPTER 2

THE FIFTH COMMANDMENT

"Honor your father and mother, that your days may be long in the land the Lord your God is giving you." These are the familiar words of the fifth commandment – a duty near the heart of God's moral law. The "second table of the law" contains commands five through ten and regulates interpersonal human relations. From the fact that God placed this particular instruction in a privileged position, we see that parent/child relations are a top priority in God's ordering of His world. He shows us that man's duty to his fellow man starts with his duty toward his parents.

Because God sovereignly chose to create the family as the original institution for human society, it holds a primary place. The institutions of church and state both rest and rely upon the foundation of the family. Thus if the family is in disarray, both church and state reflect that disorder. But when the family is healthy and happy, both the church and the state benefit tremendously. Stability in the family circle bears fruit throughout human society.

The fifth commandment is essential for defining the family and its functions. Among other things, this law presupposes the normative arrangement established by God at the creation. One man married to one woman is God's unchanging paradigm for

marriage. The two were made for one another, and in His goodness God joins them together and makes the two become one
flesh. Offspring from this lifelong marital union fill the world.
With the help of his wife and children, man goes forth to subdue
the earth and to rule over the creatures, for God's glory and the
good of the created order.

For a family to function properly, parents must wisely exercise
their God-given authority. God delegated authority to them and
expects them to use it with prudence, love and restraint. When
parents discipline and instruct their sons and daughters in the
early years, they train the children up in the way they should go.
Through God's blessing on careful training and loving nurture,
children can grow into responsible and faithful adults. When
they leave the parental nest and enter the world, they take all their
training with them. Yet although they leave, they never cease to
be children of their parents, governed and guided by God's command to "honor your father and mother, that your days may be
long in the land which the Lord your God is giving you."

As we know all too well, sin entered the world through our
first parents and disrupted the family immediately. When God
prosecuted Adam for his covenant breaking act, Adam played the
coward by blaming his wife whom God had given him. Not long
afterward, tragedy tore apart the first family on earth as Cain mur-
dered his brother Abel, and was driven away from his home. Since
that time, families experience the effects of the fall as parents
alternately neglect or oppress their children, and children rebel
against their parents. Fallen human beings are not inclined to
honor father and mother. Their sinful natures pull them in the
opposite direction. Thus, the saving grace of God through Christ
is entirely necessary if anyone is to keep the fifth commandment.
Only through the power of Christ can we honor our parents as we
ought. If God does not give us grace, we will despise and abuse
our parents. Therefore salvation by grace alone through faith

alone must be presupposed in order for us to live according to God's word.

This commandment begins with an interesting word deliberately chosen: "Honor." It is the Hebrew term *kaved*. Philip Ryken explains the meaning of this term when he writes, "The word is *kaved*, which is the Hebrew for 'heavy' or 'weighty.' It is the word the Old Testament uses for the glory of God, for the weightiness of His divine majesty. To honor one's parents, therefore, is to give due weight to their position. It is to give them the recognition they deserve for their God-given authority. To honor is to respect, esteem, value, and prize fathers and mothers as gifts from God." (Ryken, Philip, <u>Exodus Saved for God's Glory</u>, Wheaton, IL: Crossway Books, 2005, p.603)

John Currid provides additional insight "That word, *kaved* in Hebrew, literally signifies 'to be weighty, heavy, of great value and worth.' The point is that the child must not take his or her parents lightly, or think lightly of them. They must be regarded with great seriousness and value. But it is more than a mere question of attitude. It is a commandment that requires obedience." (Currid, John, <u>Exodus Volume 2</u>, Darlington, England; Evangelical Press, 2001, p.44)

Although commonly perceived to be instructions for little children, this law has bearing on children of all ages – even adult children of aging parents. Admittedly, grown children living on their own are no longer under their parent's authority. When a son or daughter marries, a new household is established and a new authority structure is recognized by God. But although adult children are not required to "obey" their parents, they are always to honor them. The weightiness of a father and a mother do not diminish with age, and adult children ought not to despise their parents.

The love that children should have toward their aging parents can show itself in respect and gratitude. A heart that is right with

God will thankfully acknowledge the Lord's goodness in providing caring parents who sacrificed on our behalf when we were small. Rather than scorning them or ignoring them in their time of need, we will seek to tangibly honor them for their years of faithful service on our behalf. Caring for an aging parent is an important way that we honor father and mother.

The specific duties required by the word "honor" are helpfully unpacked by the Westminster Larger Catechism in question and answer 127:

> **Q. 127. *What is the honor that inferiors owe to their superiors?***
> A. The honor which inferiors owe to their superiors is, all due reverence in heart, word, and behavior; prayer and thanksgiving for them; imitation of their virtues and graces; willing obedience to their lawful commands and counsels; due submission to their corrections; fidelity to, defense, and maintenance of their persons and authority, according to their several ranks, and the nature of their places; bearing with their infirmities, and covering them in love, that so they may be an honor to them and to their government.

Many of these exhortations have direct application to the lives of godly adult children of aging parents. Adult children are to demonstrate "all due reverence in heart, word and behavior." This suggests respect shown toward aging parents, even if the parent does not always conduct himself or herself respectably.

Surely it is the proper place of children to pray for their parents with thanksgiving. Even from a great geographical distance, prayer for an aging parent is powerful and important. As the adult child prays, he ought to give thanks for the many kindnesses God has shown to and through his parent. Prayer with thanksgiving is a great antidote to a complaining spirit that is overburdened with the weight of giving care and making difficult decisions.

Because children bear the likeness of their parents, they should imitate their virtues and graces. Even the worst parent has some good qualities that could be imitated. Though adults should never follow their parents in sinful ways, they can joyfully pattern their conduct after the many good aspects of their parents' examples. Adult children should study their parents' priorities and conduct. Considering the outcome of their conduct, adult children should imitate the faith of Christian parents.

Another way that adult children honor their parents is to manifest due submission to their corrections. Children are not always right and parents are not always wrong – even late in life. Though a parent of an adult child does not wield the same authority as earlier in life, he or she can still give wise counsels and godly rebukes to erring children. How much trouble would have been avoided if the priest Eli had done more with his wayward sons, and if they had heeded their father's discipline.

One of the most important responsibilities of an adult child is to show fidelity to, defense and maintenance of their parents' persons and authority. Respecting means standing up for them and their honor, especially when the parent is no longer able to do so for himself or herself. As an aging parent is increasingly feeble and infirm, they need their children to loyally defend them. Abuse of the elderly is increasingly common, and adult children can be a strong line of defense against unscrupulous people who would prey upon the weak and helpless. So, too, the adult child must provide maintenance for their parents.

Finally, it is good to bear with the infirmities of our parents and cover them in love. An indolent son will call his parent's faults to the attention of others, and to join in ridicule and mockery of the parent. But a devoted child will cover over the faults and failings of the parent. 1 Peter 4:8 clearly applies: "Above all, keep fervent in your love for one another, because love covers a multitude of sins."

Before we end our consideration of the fifth commandment, we ought to recognize that it is the only one of the ten that contains an explicit promise. Paul refers to it as "the first command with a promise" in Ephesians 6:2. The promise is found in the words "so that it may be well with you, and you may live long on the earth." Two implications emerge from this promise. The first is that those who honor their parents will live well and live long on the earth. They will experience God's blessing in their lives, because they honored their father and mother.

The second implication is a negation of the first – those who dishonor their parents will neither live well nor live long on earth. The same point is made in Proverbs 30:17 "The eye that mocks a father and scorns a mother, the ravens of the valley will pick it out, and the young eagles will eat it."

If for no other reason than selfish preservation, an adult child should honor his father and mother. This promise and its threatening corollary are meant to motivate us to do what God commands. Human beings naturally want to live long and happy lives. A key to such an existence is faithful obedience to the fifth commandment. When we humbly live according to God's word and become faithful doers of the word, we find ourselves blessed in what we do. But those who disregard the clearly revealed will of God in Scripture should expect no such blessing upon their life.

Questions for Discussion

- Why is the fifth commandment important for human society?
- What does the fifth commandment tell us about the family?
- How did sin impact the family? What is needed for people to keep the fifth commandment?
- What is the meaning of the Hebrew word Kaved?
- Are adult children still required to honor their parents? Why or why not?
- What does the Westminster Larger Catechism Q&A 127 say to adult children? How do these duties apply to your situation?
- What is the promise given in the fifth commandment? Why is that significant for adult children of aging parents?

CHAPTER 3

BIBLICAL EXAMPLES PRO AND CON

I n His infinite wisdom, God has given us both commands and examples in His holy word. The commands lay out the principles, while the examples illustrate what the concept is supposed to look like in real life. Propositional truths need stories to show us how to apply the commandment in our own experience. Some examples are positive in nature, while others are "counter-examples." The negative examples show us how we ought not to behave. Both types of examples serve to flesh out the truth in its fullness.

Illustrating the fifth commandment are numerous Scriptural examples of both a positive and negative character. One account containing both positive and negative examples is found in Genesis 9:20-29. After Noah departed the ark, he began farming in the cleansed creation. He planted a vineyard, harvested his grapes, made some wine and partook of the fruit of his labor. Indeed, father Noah consumed enough to become drunk, and he shamed himself by uncovering himself inside his tent. At this point in the story, Noah displayed infirmity and dearly needed someone to cover over it in love.

Noah's youngest son, Ham came upon the shocking scene. When Ham saw the nakedness of his compromised parent, Ham failed to cover over the sin. Instead, he told his brothers outside. While it is not entirely obvious from the text what his youngest son "had done to him," Noah was clearly aware and infuriated when he awoke. What is clear is that Ham dishonored his parent rather than bearing with and covering over the infirmity.

In sharp contrast is the conduct of Noah's other sons – Shem and Japheth. When these two brothers heard of their father's plight, they worked together to address the situation. They took a garment and laid it upon both of their shoulders, walking backward into the tent in order to cover their father's nakedness. The text emphasizes that their faces were turned backward so that they did not see Noah's nakedness.

In this action they show the prudence of godly men who hear of parental infirmity and quickly act in a way that maintains his dignity. Their respect was evident for the man who had not only given them birth, but had saved their lives through his righteous obedience to God. Their father had stood alone in a very corrupt generation and had been a preacher of righteousness to a depraved culture. He deserved honor, not mockery. Shem and Japheth displayed their fidelity to, maintenance and defense of his good name and reputation. They loved their father in a very practical way!

As an interesting outcome of this situation we see that the child that scorned his father was cursed – he and his descendants after him for many generations. But the result is quite different for godly Shem and his holy brother Japheth – these two were blessed for their service to their parent. It is not too much to conclude that those who truly honor their aging parents will have long and fruitful lives upon the land which the Lord gives them, but those who despise and disdain their parents can harbor no such hopes. A cursed existence follows those who dishonor mother or father.

Another early Scriptural example is that of Joseph and Jacob. When Joseph finally revealed himself to his brothers in Genesis

45, his first question was "Is my father still alive?" Upon receiving assurances that Jacob yet lived, Joseph dispatched his brothers to Canaan: "Hurry and go up to my father, and say to him, 'Thus says your son Joseph, "God has made me lord of all Egypt; come down to me, do not delay. ¹⁰ "You shall live in the land of Goshen, and you shall be near me, you and your children and your children's children and your flocks and your herds and all that you have. ¹¹ "There I will also provide for you, for there are still five years of famine *to come,* and you and your household and all that you have would be impoverished." '

When a revived Jacob finally arrived in Egypt, their reunion was beautiful. Genesis 46:29-30 records the scene: "Joseph prepared his chariot and went up to Goshen to meet his father Israel; as soon as he appeared before him, he fell on his neck and wept on his neck a long time. ³⁰ Then Israel said to Joseph, "Now let me die, since I have seen your face, that you are still alive."

When Jacob drew near death, he secured a pledge from Joseph that he would be buried with his fathers in Canaan rather than with foreigners in Egypt. Joseph then arranged and choreographed an interview between his aged father and Pharaoh. Later, when word came that Jacob was ill, Joseph took his two sons to see Jacob. All the while Joseph had been providing food and lodging for his father and their extended family. Joseph was a dutiful son with a deep attachment to his father.

When Jacob died, Joseph was there to weep over his dead body. Joseph then took steps to keep his promise to Jacob and provide an honorable burial. The funeral cortège was so impressive that the Canaanites marveled. Joseph had honored his father in life and in death, and that was not lost on the pagan neighbors.

Perhaps a classic example of honoring a parent is found in the sweet book of Ruth. Having lost her husband and her sons to death, Naomi was a woman with a bitter life. She had lost all hope, and was preparing to live out her days in self-pity. Her daughter-in-law Ruth was a woman of excellent character. By remaining with Naomi, and caring for her, Ruth brought joy back into Naomi's blighted existence. Ruth's commitment was clearly voiced when she told Naomi in Ruth 1:16-17, "Do not urge me to leave you *or* turn back from following you; for where you go, I will go, and where you lodge, I will lodge. Your people *shall be* my people, and your God, my God. Where you die, I will die, and there I will be buried. Thus may the LORD do to me, and worse, if *anything but* death parts you and me." At the end of the book, when Naomi holds Boaz and Ruth's baby in her lap, the people of Bethlehem testify that Ruth has loved her and been better than seven sons to Naomi.

The final example needs some introductory explanation. Jesus Christ was and is the eternal son of God. In the incarnation He took on a true human nature and became fully man and fully God – in two distinct natures and one person, forever. As God incarnate, He is the only redeemer of God's elect. His redemptive work is unique and unrepeatable – especially by sinful human beings. In this respect we cannot follow His example – He is beyond imitation.

With that in mind, we can properly understand how he also serves in other respects as an example for his people. Without denying or diminishing his deity, Peter holds up Christ as an example for believers. He writes in 1 Peter 2:21 "For you have been called for this purpose, since Christ also suffered for you, leaving you an example for you to follow in His steps." Jesus is not merely an example, or only an example, but He is always the perfect example for the people He redeemed with His own blood.

When we consider the example of Christ toward his parents, we find precious little information about his interactions with Joseph and Mary. Joseph disappears from view sometime after the trip to the temple when Jesus was twelve. Mary shows up now and again, but is hardly a central figure in the gospels. Thus the data from

Jesus' interactions with his human parents is sketchy. We find in Luke 2:51 that he continued in subjection to them. He aids his mother at the wedding of Cana in John 2. Finally in John 19:26-27, Jesus provides for his mother's care as he is dying upon the cross. By committing her into John's care, he insured that she would be protected. However, that nearly exhausts the information about Jesus' direct connection to his own mother and father.

There is another source of information which is richer and fuller. Jesus related with reverence and submission to His heavenly Father. We see this demonstrated in John 17 as Jesus speaks directly to His Father in prayer. Recall that the Hebrew word for honor is kaved – the same word used for glory. It is not a huge step to say that when Jesus is glorifying the Father, He is honoring Him. It does not change the meaning of v.1, for instance to say "Father, the hour has come; honor Your Son, that the Son may honor you." To glorify and to honor are very closely connected concepts.

This is especially helpful in v.4 of that chapter when he says, "I glorified you on the earth, having accomplished the work which You have given Me to do." How did Jesus bring glory to the Father? How did He honor His Father? He glorified the Heavenly Father by accomplishing the work which the Father had assigned the Son. In other words, The Son obeyed the Father's command, and did what the Father had told Him – thus the Son glorified and honored His Father and showed it through in His obedience.

The respectful obedience of the Messiah had been prophesied in Psalm 40:7-8 "Then I said, "Behold, I come; In the scroll of the book it is written of me. ⁸ I delight to do Your will, O my God; Your Law is within my heart." When Jesus was conversing with the woman at the well in John 4, he told his disciples "My food is to do the will of Him who sent Me, and to accomplish His work." It is no exaggeration to say that Jesus entire earthly ministry was concentrated upon honoring His Father in heaven. He was consumed with zeal for glorifying His Father. This animated His life – it delighted His soul – it satisfied Him more than any earthly food could ever satisfy a hungry stomach.

Because Jesus was focused upon honoring and glorifying His Father, he could properly ask the Father to "glorify Your Son, that the Son may glorify You." "Now, Father, glorify Me together with Yourself, with the glory which I had with you before the world existed." Glory and honor flowed back and forth between God the Father and God the Son. As the Son honored the Father, so the Father honored the Son. Love was freely expressed as God the Father esteemed His only begotten Son, and as the Son respected and reverenced the Father of Mercies!

Not only did Jesus fully keep the fifth commandment toward both his earthly parents and His Heavenly Father, He did so for all His people. His active obedience to this and every other command are imputed to us and received by faith alone. This is THE excellent example for us to follow. If we want to know what it means to honor father and mother, we need look no further than our Savior and how He perfectly obeyed.

Questions for Discussion

- What is the relationship between commands and examples in Scripture?
- Looking at Genesis 9:20-29, what do you see about the need of an older parent? About the reactions of Noah's children?
- What was the outcome for Ham and his descendants? For Shem and Japheth?
- What does this example teach us about honoring an elderly parent?
- What principles can you draw from Joseph's care for his father Jacob?
- How does the story of Naomi and Ruth help show healthy interactions between fellow believers?
- What do we know about Jesus' relationship to his earthly parents?
- How does Jesus demonstrate honor toward His Heavenly Father? How can this pattern help us?

CHAPTER 4

NEW TESTAMENT PASSAGES AND PRINCIPLES

Having looked at the fifth commandment and several biblical examples from the Old Testament, we next turn our attention to New Testament passages and principles. We want to look at three specific passages with direct bearing upon the caring for aging parents, and then draw conclusions from them.

The first passage is from Mark 7:9-13, which reads "He was also saying to them, "You are experts at setting aside the commandment of God in order to keep your tradition. [10] "For Moses said, 'HONOR YOUR FATHER AND YOUR MOTHER'; and, 'HE WHO SPEAKS EVIL OF FATHER OR MOTHER, IS TO BE PUT TO DEATH'; [11] but you say, 'If a man says to *his* father or *his* mother, whatever I have that would help you is Corban (that is to say, given *to God),*' [12] you no longer permit him to do anything for *his* father or *his* mother; [13] *thus* invalidating the word of God by your tradition which you have handed down; and you do many things such as that."

In this passage Jesus is speaking directly to the Jews of his day about their hypocritical practices. He accuses them of setting aside God's commandments in order to maintain their own traditions.

To drive home His point, He shows how they sidestep the fifth commandment for their own selfish gain.

In verse 10, Jesus quotes two specific passages – Exodus 20:12 and 21:17. Taken together, the message is very strong for honoring father and mother. He then contrasts the clear instruction of God's word with their current practice. Claiming that financial assets were "Corban" – given to God – they no longer permitted anything to be done for the support of father and mother. By this sleight of hand, the Jews invalidated the word of God by their traditions.

This passage establishes the ongoing validity of the fifth commandment as related to the maintenance and care of aging parents. One cannot imagine that five year old children would pull such tricks to avoid giving their allowance money to mom or dad. These are the ploys of crafty adults who wish to hoard their wealth and deny their parents any financial assistance.

Jesus clearly disapproves of such stratagems, seeing them as nothing less than an invalidation of God's commandments. For an adult to find ways to neglect parental needs while covering their tracks with apparent piety is a great evil. Jesus' denunciation or such schemes is scathing.

The next passage we wish to consider would appear to be counter-productive, at least on the surface. Speaking to his disciples in Luke 14:26, Jesus states, "If anyone comes to Me, and does not hate his own father and mother and wife and children and brothers and sisters, yes, and even his own life, he cannot be My disciple." At face value, it appears that believers in Christ must "hate" their parents, as well as the rest of their family. A superficial reading would obviously contradict the fifth commandment, which cannot be the case.

The point our Lord was making is one of comparison. In the hierarchy of relational commitments, no human being can ever hold a higher place than Jesus. Believers must love Christ above and beyond every other person. If a person's primary commitment is to anyone except Jesus, then he cannot be a true disciple of Jesus. Jesus calls for undivided devotion from his followers – a complete commitment that tolerates no competition.

Rather than weakening the case for caring for aging parents, this saying of Jesus actually strengthens the duty. The outworking of our commitment to Christ includes a commitment to honoring and serving our earthly parents. Knowing that Jesus holds the primary place in our lives, we are free to love and assist a needy father or mother. We understand that we must not idolize our parent nor allow any human being to usurp Jesus' rightful place in our hearts. Neither can we neglect nor abuse our parent, realizing that Jesus will hold us accountable for how we treat the parents He assigned to us.

The third passage of importance is in 1 Timothy 5:1-8 and 16. This passage begins with counsel on how to communicate with those older than we are. In counseling his young protégé, Paul urges him to avoid sharply rebuking an older man, but to appeal to him as a father. Likewise we are to appeal to older women as mothers. The advice presupposes a natural understanding of how you would normally talk to your own biological parent. Realizing that you are still their child, you would speak respectfully to your parent. A harsh and overbearing approach toward a parent would be repugnant. In the same way, younger folk should treat older people with that same deference.

Paul then goes on to address the question of widows. This was a live issue in the early church, as seen in Acts 6:1-6. James includes the care of widows as an integral component of "pure and undefiled religion," reflecting the Old Testament emphasis on orphans, widows and aliens (cf. Deuteronomy 10:18; 26:12-13).

In a prudent way, Paul distinguishes between those who are "widows indeed" and those widows who have children or grandchildren. Christian widows without children or grandchildren had no family support network and would naturally rely on the church. These women have been left alone, have fixed their hope on God and continue night and day in prayer. The church must provide material assistance to such godly women.

If this widow is over sixty years of age, and has met the qualifications of an exemplary life of godly service, she can be put on the list. What this "list" entails is somewhat uncertain, but George Knight's conclusion seems entirely reasonable. He writes, "So a church may have a list of elderly and godly widows who have no one else to care for them and who commit themselves to serving Christ. The church commits itself to assist these widows and in turn may ask them to perform certain tasks as need arises." (III George W. Knight. The Pastoral Epistles Kindle Locations 3843-3845. Kindle Edition)

The norm for widows, however, is emphasized in vv.4, 8 and 16. When a widow has living family members, it is their responsibility to care for and assist their mother or grandmother. Paul speaks of this as "learning to practice piety in regard to their own family and make some return to their parents." Such practical piety toward your own parents is regarded as paying what is due. Knight argues that the Greek terms here mean to "return" or "recompense" and are used with the idea of "repayment". The last word "means generally 'give back,' 'restore,' 'return,' and when, as here, it is used with dative of the person and accusative of the thing, it especially means 'render what is due.'" Because it is a present tense infinitive, it has an ongoing aspect – to "keep on giving back," as noted by A.T. Robertson. (A.T. Robertson, Word Pictures of the New Testament, 1 Timothy 5:4, E4 Group Edition) The whole combination "communicates forcefully the continued obligation 'to repay what they owe' (NEB). Repayment given to parents and grandparents is in a sense a returning of the care the children received from them." (Knight. Pastoral Epistles; Kindle Locations 3757-3763)

Furthermore, to offer support for an aging family member is to provide for your own – an arrangement so usual and ordinary that even unbelievers follow this pattern. To neglect this duty would be a sin contrary to both nature and grace, and would put a professing believer in an unenviable category. According to v.8, such a person has "denied the faith and is worse than an unbeliever." Knight describe the situation as follows: "Here Paul expresses the terrible implications of not caring for one's own: It amounts to a denial of Christianity and an action and attitude worse than that of an unbeliever." (Knight. Pastoral Epistles; Kindle Locations 3807-3808)

The sin of refusing to care for a needy family member is so serious that it constitutes a practical apostasy from Christianity. Again, Knight is helpful in his comments: "Thus for a professed believer who has God's law ("honor your father and your mother") to fail to do what even many unbelievers instinctively do warrants the verdict that he is "worse than an unbeliever." (Knight. The Pastoral Epistles (Kindle Locations 3825-3826)

At the end of the section, Paul returns to the point again, saying in v.16, "If any woman who is a believer has *dependent* widows, she must assist them and the church must not be burdened, so that it may assist those who are widows indeed." Let the family be the first to provide assistance and give care to dependent widows. A Christian woman with a needy mother or grandmother <u>must</u> assist them. In God's sight, she has no other option and no greater duty.

Meanwhile, let the church come to the aid of those without networks of family support. Practically speaking, this situation makes perfect sense. No congregation has infinite resources to provide for the needs of every single widow. There simply are not enough volunteers to be available around the clock for everything every elderly member may need. Nor are the financial resources of a congregation able to continually bear the burden of providing for all of the widows in the church's membership. Recognizing our

God-given limitations, the church rightly should expect the family to bear the burden of caring for their own. The church can then handle those special cases without adequate means of support.

Finally, the church has a duty to explain and prescribe these things. If the church does not use her teaching ministry to expound the word of God on this matter, how will people know what to do? In our day, the default response is to turn to the civil government for care. "Surely a government program must exist to help me," is the usual reaction to a crisis. When the elderly become dependent on an agency of the government, the Biblical solution of family and church is subverted.

Civil governments are necessary for certain needs of the citizenry, and the magistrates can provide valuable service in their proper spheres of responsibility. God has ordained their existence and delegated certain matters to them. Although it is universally assumed to be true, it is unproven and unprovable that civil government is tasked to care for the elderly. This mercy ministry belongs first to the family and second to the church. Sadly, too many families and too many churches have thoughtlessly ceded these responsibilities to federal, state or local government agencies.

If a looming crisis in care for the elderly is to be averted, families and churches must work together to quietly resume their proper role in caring for their aging family members. If this were to happen, the quality of care would quickly improve and God's blessing would rest upon both care givers and care receivers. 1 Timothy 5:4 says that giving care to our needy family members is "acceptable" or "pleasing" to God. Knight observes that "The sense of the word here is that God welcomes this activity." (Knight. Pastoral Epistles; Kindle Locations 3765-3768) What God welcomes, He surely blesses and prospers!

Questions for Discussion

- What tendency did Jesus identify in Mark 7:9-13, and how did He evaluate it?
- What does Jesus require of those who would be His disciples in Luke 14:26? What is the positive implication of this verse for Christians?
- What does 1 Timothy 5:1-2 teach us about communication? How can this help your communication with those older than you?
- What is the difference between widows, and "widows indeed"? Can you think of examples in your own experience?
- Who is supposed to take care of the "widows indeed"? How might this be handled, practically speaking?
- What are the duties of children and grandchildren toward needy family members?
- What is the warning for those who neglect their own family?
- What is the role of the civil government in this matter? What should the family and the church do in our current situation?

CHAPTER 5

A TEAM OF HELPERS

God loves teamwork. Perfect cooperation has been His way from eternity past. Within the blessed counsel of the Trinity, Father, Son and Holy Spirit have ever worked in full agreement and sweet harmony. Jesus testified to this in John 5:19 "Truly, truly, I say to you, the Son can do nothing of Himself, unless *it is* something He sees the Father doing; for whatever the Father does, these things the Son also does in like manner."

It is no surprise that when God made the human race, He immediately instituted marriage as the usual situation. It was not good for man to be alone, so God made a helper suitable to the man. From this union God brought forth more helpers – children who were to honor and obey their parents. Together, the family is the building block of human society.

The ideal for family life is godly cooperation. Husbands are to love their wives, and wives are to love their husbands and children. Children, too, are to demonstrate their love for their parents by living in willing submission to parental authority and leadership. When the family grows older, and children become adults – even then there should be an atmosphere of kindness and cooperation.

When it comes to the care of aging parents, teamwork is a key concept. The best situation exists when a team of helpers combines their energies and abilities to serve an older member of the family circle. There are many reasons for utilizing a team approach.

First, Proverbs reminds us that there is wisdom in a multitude of counselors. No single individual can understand every aspect of a situation. Different perspectives can work in a complementary fashion to provide a fuller appreciation of the problem, as well as suggesting various ways to solve the problem.

A second reason that teamwork is valuable is the stress involved in caring for an aging parent – especially when severe mental challenges or physical illnesses exist. Often these situations demand attention literally around the clock. If an adult child has a family of his own, and job responsibilities, then taking care of an aged family member can overwhelm everything else. Difficult tasks become more manageable when others can bear the burden for a time.

Yet another reason for employing a cooperative approach is because many people rightly share the responsibility and may desire to help the loved one. If there are siblings, they each have a personal duty to honor their parents. While practical issues such as geographical distance may pose challenges, that fact does not exempt that child from caring for their parent.

A final reason for embracing a team approach is because of gifts and abilities. My own situation illustrates the point perfectly. I am a pastor and my brother is a financial advisor. I realize that my brother has talents and experience in financial matters that I lack. He may be of service to our parents in ways I cannot and should not attempt. It is no shame for me to rely upon him for help in areas of his expertise, while he could turn to me for areas where I have greater knowledge. In His wisdom God made both the family and the church to be like bodies – each member uniquely qualified to do his or her part. No two members are exactly alike. They work best when they cooperate in recognition of each other's gifts and graces.

The question then becomes, who makes up the team of helpers? We begin with those directly addressed in the fifth commandment. "Honor your father and your mother..." is aimed directly at the biological children of a husband and his wife. Adult children bear the most direct and obvious responsibility for honoring their aging parent. Naturally connected are the spouses of the adult children – the sons-in-law and daughters-in-law. If spouses are generally supposed to serve one another, it makes perfect sense that they would help out with aging in-laws. Conversely, if a spouse is unwilling to support an adult child in the care of needy relatives, the weight becomes unbearable.

Also directly involved are the grandchildren. This is directly stated in 1 Timothy 5:4 "if any widow has children or grandchildren, they must first learn to practice piety in regard to their own family and to make some return to their parents; for this is acceptable in the sight of God." Grandchildren have a duty to learn to practice piety in regard to their own family. Caring for an aging grandparent is Biblically required, and is pleasing in the sight of God. If done with a cheerful attitude, the grandparent/grandchild relationship can be especially rewarding for both parties.

As grandparents age, and their grandchildren grow up, the spouses of the grandchildren can be part of the team. I remember with great fondness visiting my wife's grandmother after we were married. On one visit, when Grandma Lou was in failing health, I had an opportunity to render service. It happened that her toilet was leaking, and I possessed a basic knowledge of plumbing. Getting down on my hands and knees, I examined the tank and discerned the source of the problem. A trip to the hardware store provided the needed part, and the difficulty was soon resolved. It gave me joy to serve that dear lady, and to make her life easier in some small way.

Another source of team members can be the local church. While the family holds a primary responsibility to the elderly, that does not prohibit church members from also lending a hand. If a congregation is to be practicing true religion, it will not neglect the elderly members in its midst. Indeed, it is the nature of the true Christian to engage in works of mercy toward those in need. When such kindness is shown to even the least person, it is done unto Christ himself (Matthew 25:34-40). Christians do this as the natural outflow of their faith, and seem blind to what they have done.

An important part of the team can be those with professional medical training. As parents age and their bodies deteriorate, specific medical problems may emerge. Sometimes these involve mental faculties, and sometimes they involve physiological systems. Having trustworthy and competent medical professionals on the team is important. Their understanding and advice cannot be discounted or ignored. With complex problems like dementia or Alzheimer's, their contribution to the team of helpers will prove invaluable.

Finally, it is often necessary for other unrelated caregivers to join the team at particular points in the process of aging. When a parent is in relatively good health and enjoys independence, then caregivers may seem unnecessary. As age advances and health declines, these unrelated caregivers may become a vital part of the team. When a loved one is moved to an institution – assisted living, a nursing home, or a care unit – then these caregivers become major players in the overall scheme. Choosing them well and cultivating good relationships with them may be important for the proper care of the family member.

Thus far we have considered how a team of helpers ought to be, but we very often face less-than-ideal situations. What are potential problems and how should we respond to them?

One problem occurs when team members refuse to participate, or do so only grudgingly. Unwillingness does not constitute grounds for an excused absence from duty. As Paul told Timothy, to neglect caring for your own family is a practical denial of the Christian faith and makes one worse than an unbeliever. If one member of the team refuses to engage, the other team members should confront that sin and call the unwilling person to repentance. If the offender staunchly refuses to repent, the task of providing care becomes even more difficult and stressful. Though you cannot make people do what they ought to do, you can lovingly address their sin and urge them to repent of it.

Another problem crops up when team members are uncooperative and argumentative. If siblings do not agree on what is best for mom and dad, they should make efforts to talk through their differences and come to a consensus. Sometimes that will entail one or the other admitting that they were wrong. Sometimes all involved may admit wrong. Where there is love between Christians, there can be true cooperation and agreement. Paul's advice to the Corinthians certainly applies: 2 Corinthians 13:11 "Finally, brethren, rejoice, be made complete, be comforted, be like-minded, live in peace; and the God of love and peace will be with you."

A vexing problem is the geographical one. When an aging parent lives many hours away, it becomes harder to maintain true cooperation. If one sibling sees the parent several times a week, and another sibling sees the parent sporadically, the capacity for true cooperation is impacted. The local sibling has daily updates on the needs and condition of the parent. The distant sibling knows only what can be gleaned from telephone calls, correspondence, or third-party reports. Given the mobile nature of modern society, this problem is likely to continue at an acute level. Easy solutions defy reason. Must the children all live geographically close to their parents? That seems as impossible to require as to enforce. Likewise, does geographical proximity necessarily mean that a local child has greater wisdom and willingness than a geographically distant child? Recognizing the challenges posed by geographical location, team members must work wisely and creatively to mini-mize that obstacle as much as possible. Communicating and un-derstanding expectations between various team members can lessen friction within the team of helpers.

A not infrequent problem is the "super sibling" who wants to do it all by himself or herself. The temptation to streamline decision-making to a single individual promises greater efficiency and less probability of conflict. Yet the individualistic approach is short-sighted and doomed to frustration and failure. What happens when the problems become complex and no obvious path rec-ommends itself? What will happen to the solitary caregiver who is already too busy with his or her own life, and now the stream of matters needing attention turns into an overwhelming flood? Ignoring the team approach will predictably produce frustration that others are not doing their fair share. It also can become a recipe for burnout through overwork. No one individual can con-tinually shoulder a heavy burden without relief and rest. Mental, physical, emotional and spiritual exhaustion are the likely destina-tion for those who insist they can and should do it all themselves.

A darker problem is termed "elder abuse." Sometimes this manifests itself in physical, emotional or verbal abuse. It can also appear as financial abuse. There is even a passive form of elder abuse in neglect. When one or more members of the team prove themselves unfit to give care, a crisis can erupt. For instance, if a sibling finds out that the caregiving sibling has been siphoning money out of the parent's checking account to pay for their own needs and wants, the family can be ripped apart and the aging parent left destitute. A similar crisis can arise when one discovers that another member of the team has physically or emotionally tor-mented the elderly parent. Legal issues can complicate an already complicated situation as the authorities enforce laws against elder abuse. These matters can be very serious and need the assistance of competent legal experts, as well as sound counseling services.

A final problem is when the abuse comes from the elderly toward those giving care. Manipulation, harsh words and violent acts can sour a situation quickly. If a child or grandchild has sacrificed to assist, and then is mistreated and maligned, they can be tempted to run away from the situation and follow a path of lesser resistance.

Teamwork is never easy in this fallen and sin-cursed world. Sin touches all men – those giving care and those receiving care. How can we keep from hopelessness and despair? As teams of helpers gather together to assist those in need, they must do so in conscious reliance on the Lord Jesus Christ. Prayerful dependence on Him for strength, wisdom, guidance and success can turn difficult situations into more manageable ones.

Questions for Discussion

- How do we know that "God loves teamwork?"
- What is the ideal for family life? How does that work out generally speaking?
- What are the reasons for a team approach to caring for aging parents? Can you think of other reasons for using a team of helpers?
- Who should be included in the team of helpers?
- What are some problems facing a team approach? How can these problems be handled?
- What has been your experience in working with others? What benefits have you seen from a team approach?

CHAPTER 6

HONORING YOUR PARENTS IN
THEIR RETIREMENT YEARS

Although the Bible says nothing about the modern condition called "retirement," there is an instance that sheds some light on how we care for our parents during their years of retirement. When Joseph welcomed his father to Egypt, the patriarch Jacob was 130 years old. Genesis 47:28 informs us that "Jacob lived in the land of Egypt seventeen years; so the length of Jacob's life was one hundred and forty-seven years." For almost two decades Joseph supported, provided and cared for his aged father. Only toward the end of that time did Jacob succumb to sickness. He was apparently in reasonably good health for his advanced years. This is what many people in our day and age know as their retirement.

After finishing their vocational work, retired people can experience decades of good health and reasonable strength. They have opportunities to pursue interests neglected earlier in life. Recreational options abound, travel is available, hobbies can be honed and relationships pursued. It seems like a golden time of life for most – a dream-like existence without the stresses of job and family.

This period of time can also pose challenges to retirees. Men especially can find it difficult to adjust to an existence without the daily routine of their work environment. Their job had defined their identity for decades, but now it is gone and they wonder who they are. Many of their social connections disappear when they are no longer going to the office every day. If they were in a position of authority previously, it can be difficult to realize that no one answers to them now. Not having a clear sense of purpose, they wonder why they get up in the morning. They can spend their days searching for activity to fill the hours. Hobbies may prove enjoyable for a time, but even these pursuits can become stale after a while.

Additional challenges face them if their spouse, friends and peers experience health problems. Suddenly their own mortality stares them in the face, and they grapple with the brevity of their own personal lives. Other physical changes crowd in on them – they are not able to do as much as they once could. The slowing pace and the lowering energy impacts their sense of vitality. They feel they are "growing old."

Relationships can be a two-edged sword. With much more time on their hands, older adults can develop relationships without distraction. Yet the relationships that mean most to them can be inaccessible. Other retired friends leave on long trips and are away for months out of the year. Children and grandchildren are busy with their own jobs and families and do not have as much time to interact. Just at a time when the older parents have ample time for visiting, children and grandchildren have diminished time for such fellowship.

Desires and expectations sometimes run contrary to experience. Parents may want to see a grown child on a regular basis. They suppose they have a right to expect this, given all they have sacrificed over the years. Yet they seldom see their child, and when they do it is only for brief periods. Frustration grows and tension results. The parent feels unfairly neglected by an over-busy child, while the child senses the parent wants more than he or she can offer. The child thinks the parent unreasonable, and forgetful of what life is like in middle age. Fear and anger can add spice to the mixture, and the relationship breaks down instead of building up.

Another element that must not be underestimated is the desire for independence and autonomy. The parents have lived their lives as independent adults, and they want to continue making all of their own decisions. Living on their own, setting their own schedules, financial autonomy and driving are all components of this independent life. To sacrifice even a small measure of independence seems like surrender, and is doggedly resisted. For a time, this works well. As long as the bills are paid, and the grass is cut, and the house is clean, nobody thinks twice about it. For adult children, this is all they've ever known. Their parents have always been capable of caring for themselves.

Then signs start to emerge that everything is not quite right. A little slip here or there indicates that capacities are waning. The child begins to notice tell-tale signs that the parent might need help. Should I offer help, or will that be perceived as an insult? How long should I let things go before I try to intervene? Things may reach an apparent tipping point and intervention seems necessary. Yet the good intentions are met with stout resistance and vicious accusations. The child backs off and has little desire to get his nose bloodied again.

A final component of this unprecedented situation might be termed "baggage carried from the past." From birth onward, parents and their children are developing relationships with one another. These relationships are a two-way street. It should not surprise us that these relationships do not always drastically improve when the child turns fifty and the parent is in their seventies. Many caregivers see the relationships continue in a more intensified form. If a parent was stubborn and argumentative in their forties, they will not usually become docile and cooperative in their seventies. Likewise, if a child was rebellious and resentful in their twenties, they do not necessarily become submissive and appreciative in their fifties. For most people, change comes gradually and incrementally. As the fruit ripens on the tree, it does not turn into an entirely different fruit – it is the same fruit, just in a riper form.

Where there is baggage from the past – include hurts from years gone by – both the aging parent and the adult child can experience God's transforming grace. They can forgive and be reconciled to one another. If a child will deal rightly with his or her own feelings, and have compassion on their needy parent, mercy can be extended and enjoyed – the relationship can heal by God's Spirit. What a good thing for a Christian parent to be truly reconciled to a Christian child, and for them to live in harmony and peace. How good and pleasant it is for them to dwell together in unity.

So what are some keys for adult children as they deal with their parent during retirement years? First of all, an adult child should put on a heart of love and compassion for their parent. Colossians 3:12-13 states, "So, as those who have been chosen of God, holy and beloved, put on a heart of compassion, kindness, humility, gentleness and patience; [13] bearing with one another, and forgiving each other, whoever has a complaint against anyone; just as the Lord forgave you, so also should you."

Without a proper attitude of affection, the relationship will be superficial at best. Grappling with your own attitudes and feelings toward your parent may be a difficult aspect of your sanctification – especially if you were hurt by your parent in the past. But love is essential for a healthy relationship. 1 John 4:10 says "In this is love, not that we loved God, but that He loved us and sent His Son *to be* the propitiation for our sins. [11] Beloved, if God so loved us, we also ought to love one another." God's love and forgiveness sets us free to love others in a godly fashion. This is needful when dealing with retired parents – no matter how good or bad the relationship has been. Love is always appropriate and always bears much good fruit.

Second, good relationships are cultivated by consistent communication over time. If months go by with little or no substantial communication between retired parents and adult children, the relationship begins to wither. We are creatures made with a God-given capacity for communication. Through the give-and-take of conversation we share in each other's lives and grow to understand and appreciate the struggles we all face. We cannot bear one another's burdens in love, and thus fulfill the law of Christ, if we never speak to each other. Given the hectic pace of modern life, such communication needs to be deliberately planned or it may not happen. Good intentions are inferior to wise plans.

A third suggestion is attentive understanding. Recognizing that retired parents value their independence means we should not callously trample on their right to direct their own lives as they see fit. They are still responsible for the choices they make and the consequences flowing from those decisions, although we may not agree with the choices they make or the priorities they maintain. Yet an attentive adult child will be ever watchful for signs that the parent may need help. In an understated way, the child can monitor the situation so as to intervene when truly needed. Knowing exactly when to step forward and how to best help is a matter that demands wisdom. If anyone lacks wisdom, they should ask God, who gives freely to all without finding fault. Such God-given wisdom may avert an unnecessary crisis, or at least lessen the damage.

Finally, adult children can gather much valuable insight from godly counselors with practical experience. Often there are older saints in the church who have gone through similar scenarios. The understanding they gleaned can keep us from making painful mistakes. Simply asking, "Have you ever faced a situation like this?" can lead to profitable discussion. "What did you do and how did it turn out?" is another good question.

Questions for Discussion

- What biblical example do we see of an adult child caring for a "retired" parent? What does it teach us?
- What are some of the challenges faced by retired people? Have you seen examples of this yourself?
- What factors can complicate the relationship between retired parents and their adult children?
- Why is the loss of independence such a significant factor for retirees? Can you give examples?
- What baggage from the past can hinder a good relationship? How can that baggage be dealt with faithfully?
- Why is love so vital for a good relationship? How do we gain a heart of compassion for a needy parent?
- What is the role of consistent communication? How would you rate yourself as a communicator?
- What is "attentive understanding?"
- Who are godly counselors that can help you as an adult child?

CHAPTER 7

DEALING WITH ILLNESS: PHYSICAL, MENTAL, EMOTIONAL, SPIRITUAL

"I'm not a doctor and I don't play one on TV..." As a pastor, I do not pretend to understand the physiological complexities of the human body. I greatly admire those who have studied medicine and devote their lives to serving others in this way.

That said, I do know certain things to be true about the physical condition. These insights come from the Word of God, rather than from medical journals. A Biblical/theological perspective on illness can be helpful to those who experience such conditions, as well as those who care for the sick. We will look at various Biblical perspectives on illness, and then consider practical issues.

The first Biblical principle is that all kinds and types of illness are the result of man's fall into sin, and are the consequences of God's curse on our first parents. Prior to their eating of the forbidden fruit, Adam and Eve did not experience bodily infirmities or decay. The perfection of Eden was shattered by their foolish choice, and illnesses of all sorts were unleashed on the world. Many of the maladies we encounter in life are simply the results of living in a fallen and sin-cursed world. Adam and Eve bear a certain responsibility for what has happened to their posterity.

A second principle is that some illnesses are directly related to sinful behavior. If a person abuses their body in violation of God's commandments, they can sometimes contract physical conditions as a result. Habitual drunkenness can destroy the liver and lead to death. Sexual immorality can expose a person to sexually transmitted diseases, such as HIV/AIDS. We ought to recognize that there can be a one-to-one correspondence between sinful choices and physical problems. In such situations, repentance is part of the proper response and "cure."

We would also recognize that some conditions are God's righteous punishment upon the sins of men – either directly or indirectly. When King Herod accepted the idolatrous adulations of the citizens of Tyre and Sidon, and failed to instead glorify God, an angel struck him down, and he was eaten by worms and died. When the Corinthians abused the Lord's Supper, they suffered physical consequences. After warning them about their dangerous behavior, Paul adds this note in 1 Corinthians 11:30: "For this reason many among you are weak and sick, and a number sleep." In the same way, King David experienced physical ramifications of his sins against Bathsheba and Uriah, testifying in Psalm 32:3-4 "When I kept silent *about my sin*, my body wasted away Through my groaning all day long. [4] For day and night Your hand was heavy upon me; My vitality was drained away *as* with the fever heat of summer." Although God does not always act in this way, He can and sometimes does afflict people as a judgment upon their sinful choices.

At other times, God sends illness upon human beings so that He might be glorified in the sight of men. An instructive passage is found in John 9. As Jesus ministered in Jerusalem, he encountered a man who was blind from birth. His disciples asked him an understandable question: "Rabbi, who sinned, this man or his parents, that he would be born blind." This question presupposes a direct connection between sin and blindness. Not unlike Job's friends, the disciples reasoned backward from the effect to the cause. Their only question was, "Who sinned? This man himself, or his parents?"

Jesus' reply is surprising: "*It was* neither *that* this man sinned, nor his parents; but *it was* so that the works of God might be displayed in him." (John 9:3) What this demonstrates is that while God sometimes punishes human sin with affliction, He does not always do so. Thus it cannot be assumed that if a person suffers from illness, they must necessarily be reaping the consequences of their sin. Often God has other purposes in mind, and alternative explanations are possible. What Jesus did for that blind man became a demonstration of His glory before the watching multitudes of Jews. It also led the blind man to faith in Jesus. After this man had been accosted by the Pharisees, Jesus searched him out. "Do you believe in the Son of Man?" he asked. The man answered, "Who is He, Lord, that I may believe in Him?" Jesus then revealed himself to the man, and the man responded, "Lord, I believe." And he worshiped Him." (John 9:38) Again, God's glory comes through as a sinner is saved through faith in Christ. That was the reason for the man's blindness – not some past sin.

We must also recognize that sometimes earthly difficulties are due to the malice of Satan. Job's story is a case in point. Unbeknownst to Job, Satan asked for and received God's permission to torment this holy man. At first the afflictions came in the form of tragic losses – oxen, donkeys, sheep, camels, servants, sons and daughters – all swept away in rapid succession. Next came physical affliction. Satan smote Job with sore boils from the sole of his foot to the top of his head. To make matters worse, the suffering saint heard foolish counsel from his own wife. She advised him to let go of his integrity, to curse God and to die. Topping it all off, three well-meaning but misguided friends showed up to sympathize with him. Their efforts to "help" only deepened Job's misery.

Behind the scenes stood Satan, leering in malice as he pressed Job hard. But behind Satan stood God, who permitted Satan to work within certain limitations. And what was God's purpose? Evidently to test Job and to refine him through suffering. As Job is falling to the ground and worshiping, he testifies to the Lord's goodness, and he blesses the name of the Lord. Throughout, Job did not sin nor did he cast blame upon his God. This was a monumental test of Job's faith in the God he worshiped and served. Often God uses sickness to test the faith of his saints.

Having recognized various Biblical themes on the causes and nature of physical afflictions, let me turn in a more positive direction. The Scriptures repeatedly teach that God is the one who "heals all our diseases." (Psalm 103:3) This is demonstrated throughout Jesus' earthly ministry in the many instances of healing. Matthew 9:35-36 provides an overview of Jesus' ministry in the following words, "[35]Jesus was going through all the cities and villages, teaching in their synagogues and proclaiming the gospel of the kingdom, and healing every kind of disease and every kind of sickness. [36] Seeing the people, He felt compassion for them, because they were distressed and dispirited like sheep without a shepherd." Jesus' ministry was not only a preaching ministry, but it included healing. Often large crowds would come to him with all of their diseased family and friends. Jesus would patiently and persistently heal each and every one of them. I recall seeing a poignant wall decoration in the waiting room of the doctor who delivered our third child. It simply stated that, "Doctors treat, God heals!" How true this is – God is the one who alone can heal.

In healing all of our diseases, God is free to work directly or indirectly, through means or apart from means. Sometimes a word spoken at a distance was sufficient to effect healing on a sufferer. But then there are cases like King Hezekiah. In Isaiah 38 we learn that the king had become mortally ill. The Lord sent a message through the prophet Isaiah that Hezekiah'would die, and should make preparations. Hezekiah wept and prayed, and God granted him fifteen more years of life. But we find that his recovery came through a specific treatment, for in v.21 we read, "²¹ Now Isaiah had said, "Let them take a cake of figs and apply it to the boil, that he may recover." Christians can and should use medical means for treatment of diseases, while recognizing that God is the one who ultimately brings about healing. To employ doctors, medicines, treatments and surgeries is not demonstrating a lack of faith. Neither is it especially holy to refuse on principle to receive treatment for a medical condition. Our stewardship of our bodies requires that we do everything we can to sustain and preserve life.

From both the Biblical data and personal experiences, we can see that illness of body often touches the mind, the emotions, the spirit and even the will of the suffering person. When one part of the body suffers, all the other parts share in its suffering. Sometimes the affliction primarily impacts the mind, which in turn can depress the emotions. As there is an organic unity to our human experience, we must admit that disease and difficulty can impact the whole person in all of his faculties.

Another reality we recognize is that the process of aging breaks down the body, frequently increasing our afflictions. They increase in variety and intensity, as slowly but surely we progress toward the day of death. The life of man, which was so vigorous and energetic in early days, fades away toward evening. The flower that bloomed so beautifully in the bright new morning is now wilted and worn toward sundown.

Compounding the challenge of disease are those well-meaning Christian friends who can sometimes react badly to illness in others, thus intensifying the suffering of the victim. Again we think of Job's three friends, who kept insisting that Job must have done something to deserve what he experienced. If only he would admit his wrongdoing, his problems could be reversed. This conventional wisdom was simply inaccurate for Job's situation. Though not perfect, Job had been blameless in his conduct and had done nothing deserving God's wrath and curse. So in addition to coping with his painful physical condition, he had to refute the "comfort" of his self-confident friends.

One last reality that we cannot deny is that medical care is often a mixed bag. Beyond doubt, doctors and nurses can possess significant amounts of medical knowledge. Their experience with similar cases gives them further advantages in treating conditions found in their patients. Yet no human being is omniscient, and no medical professional knows everything about any one area of medicine. Neither can even the most expert specialist know infallibly what is happening within a patient's body or mind. So although we greatly appreciate modern medicine, we can also recognize its limitations. There are certain conditions that exceed the knowledge and ability of medical professionals.

Once during Jesus' ministry he encountered a woman whose experience is instructive. Mark 5:25-26 records the particulars: "A woman who had had a hemorrhage for twelve years, [26] and had endured much at the hands of many physicians, and had spent all that she had and was not helped at all, but rather had grown worse" This woman came up behind Jesus, touched his cloak in faith, and was instantly healed by his power. It is telling that she had endured much at the hands of many physicians. It had cost her everything she had, but her condition only deteriorated. She received no help at all, until she came to Jesus. I include this account not to denounce medical professionals or discourage treatment, but simply to show that we cannot put blind faith in medical professionals. They are not worthy of absolute trust and utter confidence. They can be of great use in many situations, but they are not God. If they are consulted and appreciated in their proper creaturely place, God can use them for the good of those who suffer. But putting modern medicine on a high pedestal and ascribing almost divine powers to its practitioners is a serious mistake.

With those principles in mind, let us now face the more practical questions for adult children caring for aging and sickly parents. What are some suggestions for helping an elderly loved one in such circumstances?

First we would remember the importance of prayer – prayer with and for the ailing family member. Not only should a caregiver offer up personal prayers, but it is appropriate to call the elders of the church to pray. James 5:14-15 asks the question, "[14] Is anyone among you sick? *Then* he must call for the elders of the church and they are to pray over him, anointing him with oil in the name of the Lord; [15] and the prayer offered in faith will restore the one who is sick, and the Lord will raise him up, and if he has committed sins, they will be forgiven him." Often when healings are recorded in the Scriptures, they are the direct answers to prayer by God's servants (cf. Genesis 20:17 and Acts 28:8).

One of the debated points in James' exhortation is the "anointing with oil." As Jesus indicates in the parable of the Good Samaritan, anointing a wound with oil was considered part of the medical treatment of that time. In this light, the prayers of the elders should be accompanied by appropriate treatment. Prayer is not a substitute for medical care, but an important corollary to visiting a doctor.

Throughout the ordeal of sickness, patience, sympathy and understanding are vital to an elderly person. Nothing is quite so miserable as being alone when you are sick. Having a friendly face at your side can cheer the heart when despair is at hand. Driving your aging parent to appointments, sitting in on the visit with the doctor, writing down the crucial information for later discussion, filling prescriptions and making sure they are taken on schedule – it can become a significant undertaking for busy adult children. Having a team to help shoulder this burden is most important.

Having your own support network is also valuable so that you are not crushed by the weight of responsibility.

Finally, knowing that God sees all you do, and approves of your service, is reassuring. Ponder Jesus' words in Matthew 25 "… I was sick, and you visited Me… 'Truly I say to you, to the extent that you did it to one of these brothers of Mine, *even* the least *of them,* you did it to Me.'"

Questions for Discussion

- Summarize the relationship between sin and disease? Biblically speaking, what are the causes of human suffering?
- As parents age, what types or categories of illness do they frequently face?
- What was Jesus' attitude toward those suffering from various sicknesses? How can his attitude help us as we encounter illness in those we care for?
- What responsibilities fall to adult children as illness touches their parents? What are the challenges of chronic sickness? Of terminal illnesses?
- What stresses arise from prolonged sickness in a parent? What are some ordinary reactions to those stresses?
- What part does prayer play in our response to sickness?
- What are specific ways to honor a parent who faces illness? How can we treat them with dignity in the midst of their suffering?

CHAPTER 8

CARING FOR THOSE WITH DEMENTIA

One of the more challenging situations facing adult children with aging parents arises when symptoms of dementia begin to appear. As the mind of the parent declines, the need for care correspondingly increases. Watching a respected father or beloved mother suffer from dementia can be mentally, emotionally, physically, spiritually and financially draining.

Readers who have a parent diagnosed with some form of dementia know far more about the condition than I do. As I freely admit, I am not medically trained and have no expertise in health care. However, it is valuable for those who do not have first-hand experience to know some general definitions and descriptions. In this chapter I wish to provide a basic introduction to various forms dementia, the most common of which is Alzheimer disease. I will then review some helpful theological insights. We will consider issues facing caregivers, and then look at several case studies.

The term "dementia" refers to a category of brain disorders causing reasoning problems and memory losses. Generally speaking, dementia is connected to changes in the size, condition and capacity of the brain. Dementia can be caused by any number or combination of factors, including age, heredity, high blood pressure, smoking, diabetes, and head injuries

There are numerous types of dementia, including Alzheimer disease, vascular dementia, Parkinson disease dementia, dementia with Lewy bodies, Frontotemporal dementia and others.

Early symptoms can include confusion, frustration, agitation, memory loss, difficulty learning new information, difficulty with communication, concentration and reasoning, an inability to perform complex tasks, losing objects, panic, withdrawal, or getting lost in familiar places. As dementia progresses, the patient may suffer from increased anger, hostility and aggression, hallucinations and delusions, emotional outbursts, inconsolable crying, disorientation, inability to perform basic tasks like eating or bathing, and incontinence.

There are presently no one-size-fits-all diagnostic medical tests for every case of dementia. Doctors evaluate on a case-by-case basis and depend on information from the patient and family members. While there is no recognized cure for dementia, treatment may include medications aimed at slowing the progression of the dementia or managing symptoms and behaviors related to the disease. As the dementia progresses, the burden of caring for the patient increases on family members, caregivers, health care professionals and society in general.

Thinking about dementia from a Biblical/theological vantage point, we would recognize that these conditions are the general effects of man's fall in Genesis 3. To suggest that dementia is God's punishment upon a person's sin, or that it comes from a lack of faith is speculative at best and insensitive and hurtful to all involved.

We would also affirm that when a believer suffers from memory loss due to some form of dementia, he does not forfeit his soul or lose his salvation. A Christian with advanced Alzheimer disease, for instance, may no longer remember what he or she believes, or be able to articulate a confession of faith in Christ. Yet such a one does not cease to be secure in the sovereign care of the Triune God. To paraphrase Paul, neither dementia nor Alzheimer disease is able to separate us from the love of God, which is in Christ Jesus our Lord.

From our general understanding of the Scriptures, we believe there is no sin in continuing the ethical research of these conditions, and working toward better treatments and possible cures. Christianity is not fatalism, which is passively resigned to our fallen condition. Historically speaking, thoughtful Christians have been on the forefront of medical care. This involvement is not in spite of our beliefs, but because of them.

So what are the issues facing caregivers attending a person suffering from dementia? One common challenge is the grief of relating to a person who no longer recognizes the caregiver's identity or their long-standing relationship. For instance, when a grown daughter cares for a mother who simply cannot understand or remember who the child is, or recall their lifelong bond, the daughter can be understandably unsettled.

Another reality is that the parent, who for all of life had been self-sufficient and self-reliant, now needs help with eating, dressing, bathing and even moving. This can be a very time consuming process, testing the patience of the caregiver. Can the caregiver slow down and provide help at the pace needed by the parent, or will impatience grow into frustration?

As the dementia progresses, the parent may go through times of irrational behaviors. They may become aggressive, temperamental, abusive, or violent. They may engage in activities that are very much out of character for them – such as stealing items from other patients at a care facility. They may become "naughty," and engage in destruction of property for no apparent reason. This can require additional commitments from the adult children that will demand money, time and attention. Hiring additional care-givers to monitor the bad behaviors may be very costly. Staying with the adult parent around the clock can create stress with job responsibilities of the adult child.

Connected to this are questions about medications. When is it necessary to administer medications that will control unwanted behavior? If the medications cause the parent to be insensible, and to sleep all the time, is that appropriate? Sometimes adult children can be conflicted about how much medication is given to the parent, and what the appropriate dosages should be.

For those who desire to care for their parent in their own home, the progress of dementia creates new complexities. Will the adult child provide all of the care? Will other siblings, or other family members take part? How much can be expected from the adult child's spouse? Should children and grandchildren be part of the team, or is that unrealistic? What about outside caregivers who are not members of the family? Who should be hired, and how should they be paid? At what point does the burden become unman-ageable and unrealistic? Is there a time to consider a healthcare facility that provides specialized care for advanced dementia? If the parent is institutionalized, what is the role for the adult child in caregiving and decision-making? How often should the adult child visit their institutionalized parent? These questions have no easy and obvious answers that fit all situations and conditions. But these questions (and many others) will arise, demanding answers.

Case Study #1: Bob and Debbie were living in northern Illinois when they first began noticing signs of trouble with Debbie's wid-owed mother. Mom was misplacing items around the house and having problems remembering where she had put them. Often when she lost an item, she would panic and become upset. Besides losing things, during conversations she was repeating herself fre-quently, and her driving skills were noticeably declining as well. Debbie and her sisters discussed their growing concerns for their mom and decided to keep a closer eye on her as well as have her examined by her physician. The forgetfulness increased as time wore on, even to the point that some extended family members, neighbors, and friends from church were also aware of her general decline. Nothing was actually done right away because the family agreed they did not want to force anything on her, but they would occasionally talk with her and make suggestions about various options.

They soon sought out help at a memory center in nearby Chicago where much neurological, psychological, and physical testing was done. They eventually received a diagnosis of Alzheimer disease. She herself knew there was something was wrong, and when the diagnosis came, she was not ashamed to tell people about her disease. She told friends from her church and many of them helped her in those early stages.

A turning point came on one of the occasions when Mom lost her purse. She had set it down somewhere, but could not recall where. Though a search was made, the purse could not be found. About a week later, Debbie was outside her mom's home when she spotted the purse sitting atop the air conditioner. Around that time, Mom also had some flooding in her basement. Things were certainly overwhelming to her at this point, so Debbie took the opportunity to ask if she was ready to give up her home. Mom agreed and there was no turning back.

Because they themselves were busy raising their children and running a business, Bob and Debbie determined they could not give her mom the full time care she needed in their own home. This was a hard decision and they sometimes wondered if they had made the right choice. Debbie's sisters were also in similar situations so they all began searching for a facility that could provide a safer environment, even though Mom pretty well had her mind made up where she wanted to live. When the time came, she went willingly into the place of her choosing, a familiar Christian residential facility that provided structure and certain services while still allowing her a measure of independence.

Around this time, Bob was able to work closely with his mother-in-law in understanding and overseeing her finances. When she requested it, they took over the management of her financial matters. She knew she needed help, and appreciated the practical assistance they gave her.

Sometime during all this, Bob & Debbie moved their family to southeastern Wisconsin, though they were back and forth often helping take Mom to appointments with her doctor, helping clear out her home after it was sold, and also just visiting. Eventually it became very obvious this facility was no longer sufficient for Mom's needs. She became increasingly disoriented and needed more directed care. By now she was no longer able to participate in the decision making process, so Debbie and her sisters decided to search for a place that would meet her needs. After checking out several options, the most suitable facility was found in Wisconsin just minutes from Bob and Debbie's new location. Factors influencing their decision included specialized dementia care, the size and layout of the facility, geographic proximity, and finances.

Because Debbie's mom was otherwise physically healthy, they realized that she could live for a significant time. Though she had financial resources, they wanted to plan wisely so she would not run out of money. As it turned out, she lived with Alzheimer disease for more than 13 years before she passed away.

During the years in Wisconsin, she received competent care from the facility and regular visits from Bob and Debbie and other family members. She gradually declined until she could no longer go out, could not attend church, and grew increasingly detached from her family relationships. Bob and Debbie saw her on a consistent basis although there came a point when she was not responsive and did not interact with them. The family recalled that when she finally died, they realized that she had really been gone for a long time. Through the years they lost her little by little.

As they reflect back on the long ordeal, Bob and Debbie saw several keys to coping with the challenges. Because they had good established relationships with Debbie's parents from earlier days, the Alzheimer years proved more manageable. Also, keeping up regular communication with Debbie's siblings provided a support network within their extended family. Their shared Christian faith was most important as they dealt with changes and challenges. Prayer played a crucial role in their loving care of a fading mother.

Debbie's mom has been gone for over 3 years, and they can fondly remember how she was before her disease. They do not dwell on the hard years of her decline, but remember the happier days. Many of the memories of their struggle have faded, and they look forward to seeing Debbie's mother in heaven.

Case study #2: Lynn and Sandy are two unmarried sisters. Lynn is a physician and Sandy is a physical therapist. Their story began about 20 years ago, when Sandy was living in the Milwaukee area and Lynn lived and worked about 90 minutes north of Milwaukee. Their parents, Don and Jackie, were also living in Milwaukee at that time. Jackie had always been a hardworking and intelligent woman. Due to some changes at her workplace, she was required to learn certain computer skills. Despite repeated training, Jackie could not catch on or retain the information. Lynn and Sandy both realized that something unusual was happening with their mother. They had testing done, and then Lynn met with the neurologist. The neurologist informed her that their mother had dementia, and would not survive more than five years. As Lynn recalled that difficult conversation, the doctor showed little compassion for either Jackie or her family.

After the initial diagnosis, Jackie's faculties gradually declined. She could no longer work, and even common household tasks grew more challenging. Forgetfulness and confusion increased.

Sandy remembers how Jackie kept saying "I'm so stupid; I'm just a burden on everyone." She felt useless and it bothered her deeply. It was a very emotional time for the whole family. Because Sandy lived nearby, she went out of her way to visit with her parents and to find things for her mom to do. She would bring her dog to the house during the day, and let Jackie do "doggy daycare." It gave Jackie purpose and helped her feel useful.

At the same time that Jackie was declining, her husband Don experienced health problems of his own. They were no longer able to help one another, and living alone was becoming increasingly unsafe. The next critical point in the process came when Lynn and Sandy concluded that Don and Jackie were no longer safe living in their home. They needed some sort of assistance.

At first they hired caregivers to come in during the day, but that was insufficient. Night time care was also needed, but that created different problems. As Lynn recalls, the cost for 24/7 caregivers from an agency in 2006 ended up around $20,000 per month. Even with both of them working, they could not afford such an expensive long-term solution. The sisters even experimented with staying with their parents on alternating nights, but that was too exhausting and complicated.

At this time Jackie experienced a significant decline of her mental faculties, with increased confusion, little sense of danger, and no judgment about practical matters. Lynn and Sandy knew that more care was needed than they could provide. The next stop for Jackie was a nursing home. The day she was admitted was "the worst day of my life," according to Lynn. When Jackie finally realized that she was staying and Lynn was leaving, she became incredibly angry. The transition to the nursing home was very rocky for everyone involved. Because Don and Jackie had different needs, they were not initially in the same facility. That caused further friction between the sisters and their parents.

Because of their medical training and work experience in health care, both Lynn and Sandy knew the pros and cons of nursing homes. They made it their goal to be there for their parents, to pay attention to the quality of care they received, and to be the vocal advocates for their mother and father. They were not afraid to speak up and to demand excellent care for their parents – a fact that probably intimidated the nursing home staff. The quality of the nursing home was reasonably good at first. But when the facility was sold, some of the staff left and the quality of care declined noticeably.

At this juncture, an opening was available for Jackie in a nearby group home. This seemed like a better option, and the sisters made the decision to move Jackie again. The group home advertised many impressive features that attracted their attention, but some of those promises never materialized. In addition, the staff at the group home were often unable to give adequate attention to all of the residents in the group. Lynn and Sandy suspected that Jackie was being neglected at times, and that other residents were causing significant problems.

It was at that point that Lynn and Sandy began to think seriously about bringing Jackie home. In 2008, their father died. Now their focus was exclusively on caring for their mom. They carefully considered the different aspects of having their mother at home. They would need to move from Lynn's house, which was unsafe for a person in Jackie's condition. That meant building a new home that was better suited for Jackie's needs. They would also have to provide qualified caregivers. Since Sandy was trained in physical therapy, she could take the lead. She reduced her work schedule in order to be available for Jackie. They also hired a qualified caregiver who could alternate with Sandy. Lynn realized that she would need to provide the financial backing for this plan, since Sandy would be working less. With much prayer, they made the decision and moved forward.

The adjustment to having Jackie at home went smoothly, but was not without challenges. At first they were able to bring Jackie to church. As she continued to decline, that became less feasible. Both sisters realized that they themselves needed the fellowship and the encouragement of church involvement, so they began alternating services. Lynn attends in the morning, and Sandy comes to evening worship. In this way, both keep growing in their faith while they continue giving of themselves to honor their mother.

It is now 20 years since Jackie's initial diagnosis. Jackie no longer knows who her two daughters are, although she recognizes that they are somehow important to her. The daughters have watched with some sadness as the mother they knew and loved has slowly disappeared. Though she is still alive, the person she used to be is not there any longer. Yet Lynn and Sandy have made caring for their mother their mission in life at this time. According to Sandy, "This is the most important thing we've ever done, the most difficult thing we've ever done, and the most blessed thing they've ever done." Lynn adds that this has been the most significant time of spiritual growth for her personally because she's had to depend on the Lord for strength, and to forsake her own independence.

Questions for Discussion

- What is the definition given of dementia? What are some common symptoms?
- What are some Biblical and theological principles that inform our understanding of dementia? Can you think of more such Biblical principles that are helpful to adult children?
- What should be the Christian attitude toward research of dementia? What might be some differences between "ethical" research and that which is "unethical"?
- What are some common challenges facing adult children with a parent suffering from dementia? Have you encountered any of these challenges?
- As you considered the case study of Bob and Debbie, what stood out about their response to Debbie's mom's dementia?
- Looking next at the case study of Lynn and Sandy, how was their situation different? What does their example show us about decision making and long-term care?
- In light of Galatians 6:2 and Philippians 2:3-4, in what ways can you as friend or fellow church member support those caring for a parent with dementia?

CHAPTER 9

COPING WITH DIFFICULT PARENTS

How wonderful life would be if every father was continually attentive, dutiful, generous, wise and selfless. Would we not rejoice if our mothers were always good and sweet and kind, full of wisdom and tender in their compassion toward their children? The idealized family fills our imaginations with warm feelings of love and joy.

Under the cold light of reality, we are faced with the truth that even the best parents are flawed, inconsistent, selfish and harsh at times. Taking off the rose colored glasses, we see our parents as they are. The picture is not altogether flattering. Sooner or later we confess that our parents can be challenging at times. And for some, the admission is really that mom or dad are chronically difficult – deeply flawed at many points.

Time does not heal all wounds. Especially when wounds are left untreated, infections can fester. Moreover, parents who were moderately difficult in mid-life can become increasingly problematic as they age. Their unattractive qualities can intensify and concentrate, producing even more bitterness and rancor. There are more than a few elderly people who have become embittered and angry in their later years. They can convey their venom to those closest to them – even to their own children.

Relational problems between parents and children are often complicated by differing spiritual conditions. If a mother or a father is not a believer in Christ, caring for them in later years can be a heartache and a grief. When that unbelieving parent is openly hostile to Christianity, the situation can seem unbearable. How is a Christian adult child of a nonbeliever supposed to care for an antagonistic parent who rejects Christ? These are not easy issues.

To begin grappling with these challenges, let's revisit the fifth commandment again – especially as it is expounded in the Westminster Larger Catechism Question and Answer 127. First we must recall that the fifth commandment requires all children to honor their father and mother, whether that parent be easy or hardened, whether they be Christian or non-Christian or anti-Christian. We should not interpret God's word to require such honor only in the easiest and most pleasant cases. All children must honor their parents, regardless of circumstances.

The Westminster Larger Catechism gives us specific suggestions as to how that must work out. It reads as follows:

Q. 127. *What is the honor that inferiors owe to their superiors?*
A. The honor which inferiors owe to their superiors is, all due reverence in heart, word, and behavior; prayer and thanksgiving for them; imitation of their virtues and graces; willing obedience to their lawful commands and counsels; due submission to their corrections; fidelity to, defense, and maintenance of their persons and authority, according to their several ranks, and the nature of their places; bearing with their infirmities, and covering them in love, that so they may be an honor to them and to their government.

According to this answer, there are seven distinct duties required of inferiors toward their superiors:

1) all due reverence in heart, word, and behavior;
2) prayer and thanksgiving for them;
3) imitation of their virtues and graces;
4) willing obedience to their lawful commands and counsels;
5) due submission to their corrections;
6) fidelity to, defense, and maintenance of their persons and authority, according to their several ranks, and the nature of their places;
7) bearing with their infirmities, and covering them in love, that so they may be an honor to them and to their government

Each of these seven duties may seem almost impossible when it comes to a difficult parent. To have reverence toward that parent, and to display it in word and behavior? To pray with thanksgiving for them? To imitate their virtues and graces? This is challenging beyond description for some, yet it is what God wants us to do. Holding grudges against a parent, or speaking ill of them to others is sinful. To fail to pray for them is inexcusable. Even the worst parent has some virtue or common grace for which we can be thankful. So although this Catechism answer may go against our very grain as human beings, it challenges us to behave with integrity toward those who may have hurt or wronged us. It calls us to return good for evil, and to overcome evil with good.

Whether we like to admit it or not, that hard-to-love parent needs someone to defend them and maintain their lives. They need their child to bear with their infirmities and cover them in love. Like Shem and Japheth did for their father Noah, an elderly parent needs that child most when the parent is least lovely – sometimes even downright embarrassing.

In the case of a difficult parent, the Scriptures give good counsel directly applicable for the Christian adult child. One of the more important passages is Paul's words in Romans 12:17-21, where he writes, "Never pay back evil for evil to anyone. Respect what is right in the sight of all men. [18] If possible, so far as it depends on you, be at peace with all men. [19] Never take your own revenge, beloved, but leave room for the wrath *of God,* for it is written, "VENGEANCE IS MINE, I WILL REPAY," says the Lord. [20] "BUT IF YOUR ENEMY IS HUNGRY, FEED HIM, AND IF HE IS THIRSTY, GIVE HIM A DRINK; FOR IN SO DOING YOU WILL HEAP BURNING COALS ON HIS HEAD." [21] Do not be overcome by evil, but overcome evil with good."

When a parent acts like an enemy, and exhibits hostility or aggression, we must not pay back in kind. Returning evil for evil is not the Christian response. Rather, doing good in tangible ways is the appropriate response. Giving food to the hungry and drink to the thirsty is the right thing. Rather than being overcome by evil ourselves, we must actively overcome evil with good.

Another instructive passage is found in the opening verses of 1 Timothy 5, where Paul counsels this: "Do not sharply rebuke an older man, but *rather* appeal to *him* as a father, *to* the younger men as brothers, [2] the older women as mothers, *and* the younger women as sisters, in all purity." Rather than giving vent to frustration, and administering a sharp rebuke, we must appeal to the older man as a father. The same can be done for older women as mothers. When that older person is our own biological parent, our communication must be respectful and gentle, not harsh and demeaning. This is true even when our parent speaks with sharpness and harshness to us. Their bad conduct does not authorize us to speak or act sinfully in retaliation. Instead, by demonstrating restraint and respect, we heap burning coals upon their head. As the proverbs remind us, a gentle answer turns away wrath. Maintaining our cool when the temper of a parent grows hot is one of the most godly responses we can give.

Yet another angle on this scenario is found in Jesus' words in Matthew 10:32-39. This passage particularly applies to Christian children of non-Christian parents. In that passage Jesus says, "Therefore everyone who confesses Me before men, I will also confess him before My Father who is in heaven. [33] "But whoever denies Me before men, I will also deny him before My Father who is in heaven. [34] "Do not think that I came to bring peace on the earth; I did not come to bring peace, but a sword. [35] "For I came to SET A MAN AGAINST HIS FATHER, AND A DAUGHTER AGAINST HER MOTHER, AND A DAUGHTER-IN-LAW AGAINST HER MOTHER-IN-LAW; [36] and A MAN'S ENEMIES WILL BE THE MEMBERS OF HIS HOUSEHOLD. [37] "He who loves father or mother more than Me is not worthy of Me; and he who loves son or daughter more than Me is not worthy of Me. [38] "And he who does not take his cross and follow after Me is not worthy of Me. [39] "He who has found his life will lose it, and he who has lost his life for My sake will find it."

While we must respect a non-Christian parent and give them honor, we cannot allow ourselves to be wooed by their unbelief. If we allow their skepticism to subvert our faith, we have denied Christ before men – a very dangerous practice. Instead, we must continue to confess Christ before an unbelieving parent. Talking to an aging relative about the gospel is a demonstration of true love for God and for that relative. Sometimes this will provoke verbal abuse from a loved one. They may vocally reject our Christian testimony, but that does not release us from the obligation to testify to Christ before men. Sometimes this will divide the family, but Jesus warned us that such divisions would come. When faced with the choice of denying Christ or forfeiting our family relationships, we must love Christ more than even a father or a mother.

As we think about the general difficulty of dealing with unco-operative parents, we can apply these Biblical principles in a broad fashion. But how do we deal with specific challenges? Let's look at four particular problems in greater detail: unbelievers, embittered parents, alienated parents and those who are depressed.

How should a Christian respond to his unbelieving mother or father? While many passages speak to our duty to share the gospel with unbelievers, one stands out as particularly applicable in these circumstances.

Hebrews 3:12-13 says "Take care, brethren, that there not be in any one of you an evil, unbelieving heart that falls away from the living God. [13] But encourage one another day after day, as long as it is *still* called "Today," so that none of you will be hardened by the deceitfulness of sin." If we discover that anyone around us has an "evil, unbelieving heart", we should be concerned. For that person – especially an elderly parent – to fall away from the living God has eternal consequences. Furthermore, as we observe the deceitfulness of sin hardening a parent, we should be alarmed. This requires us to be attentive to the spiritual state of our parents (as well as others we regularly contact).

What should be done if we know that a parent is in such a condition? First we must "take care." The Greek verb means "to see, to take heed, to see to something, to take care." We must not close our eyes to the unbelieving heart of an aging parent. Neither should we take a fatalistic approach, as if they are beyond God's reach. Sharing the gospel with them should be a priority for the Christian child.

Not only should the believing child keep his eyes on his unbelieving parent, but he or she should daily encourage and exhort that parent. This requires not merely the "silent witness" of a faithful life, but a verbal witness spoken to the ears of the parent. Even if the parent is resistant, hostile or abusive, the child should proclaim the truth about Christ to that parent.

This spoken witness should come in a spirit of love and sincere concern for their eternal welfare. Proclaiming the gospel out of anger, frustration or spite will undermine the very message we share. While sin is deceiving and hardening the parent, the child can and should be an agent for God's truth. This truth can set free the person who has been a life-long slave to sin. By our words and by our deeds, we make the love of Christ known to unbelievers. When we live a consistent life, our gospel witness is irrefutable.

In consistently proclaiming the good news of Christ, we should remind that aging loved one that "Today is the day of salvation." While they are alive, the offer is open to them. If they were to die in their sins, then they will stand before the judgment seat of Christ to answer for their lives, their actions, their words and their refusal to heed the good news. But if they are still alive, there is still opportunity and hope. Until the day the parent dies, Christian children should not stop pointing them to the only Savior of sinners.

Another type of difficulty involves bitterness. Sometimes this feeling arises from real situations, and other times it comes from imagined injuries. Bitterness can migrate from one object to another. Bitterness toward a caregiver can morph into bitterness against family members. Often the bitterness is groundless and the harsh treatment of its victim is undeserved.

A variety of temptations can appeal to the adult child of an embittered parent. One reaction is to be angry, nasty and bitter in return. This approach assumes that "giving them a taste of their own medicine" might do some good. Another reaction is to ignore and neglect the parent because the bitterness is so unattractive. Still others might resort to gossip – as if "getting this off my chest" will help resolve the problem. Tale-bearing is never a Biblical solution to the problem of bitterness.

The author of Hebrews gives timely counsel in the 12th chapter. There he says, "[15] See to it that no one comes short of the grace of God; that no root of bitterness springing up causes trouble, and by it many be defiled;" Bitterness is like a root that springs up in the soil of the human heart. As it grows, it produces very predictable fruit. The fruit of bitterness "causes trouble." Note that it does not solve problems or resolve difficulties. Rather, bitterness spawns troubles. Moreover, bitterness defiles many. It is like a contagious disease that spreads to others and makes them sick.

So how should a child relate to an embittered parent? Point them to the grace of God as a first priority. If God has been so very gracious to you, should you not be gracious to those around you? If you think you have cause to feel embittered toward those who have wronged you, does not God have even greater reason to be bitter toward your many failings and flaws? Grace is a powerful antidote to all sin – especially to the sin of bitterness.

Along with a strong appeal to God's grace, it is appropriate to warn a person against the "root of bitterness springing up to cause trouble and defile many." I know an older widow who is regularly tempted toward bitterness. Whenever she begins complaining to me about "so-and-so" and what wrong they did to her, I look her in the eye and remind her, "Do not let bitterness grow up in your heart." To her credit, she often stops complaining and agrees with me. She knows that she is prone to bitterness, and how damaging it can be. When I voice that reminder to her, it helps her let go of her grievances.

A third issue is alienation. As people grow older, their circle of relationships will naturally dwindle. When a spouse, friends and neighbors die, the survivors can experience increasing isolation from human contact. With the isolation comes a sense of being alienated from life. This is often compounded by self-inflicted alienation over the years of life. When a parent feels alienated from those around him or her, they can become anti-social and withdrawn. What interaction they do maintain grows increasingly caustic. What is a child to do? Once again the good news of the gospel applies.

Consider Colossians 1:21-22 "And although you were formerly alienated and hostile in mind, *engaged* in evil deeds, [22] yet He has now reconciled you in His fleshly body through death, in order to

present you before Him holy and blameless and beyond reproach."
When God's grace touches a person's life, many important problems are resolved. The guilt of sin is forgiven, the stain of sin
is washed away, the wrath of God is appeased, and the sinner is
released from his slavery to sin. Not to be overlooked is the recon-
ciliation that takes place. Through Christ's death upon the cross,
the sinner is reconciled to God and the previous alienation is removed. Though we were formerly hostile toward God, our neigh-
bor, and even ourselves, we are now reconciled. The alienation is
replaced by loving acceptance. Because of the grace of God we
can now enjoy open fellowship and loving relationships with God
and with our fellow believers. We can love our neighbors as ourselves, because the alienation is removed.

One final specific problem is depression. Admittedly, this is
a huge issue experienced by many seniors. Some depression is
"clinical" and may be the result of biochemical imbalances. Such
serious cases need professional attention from trained medical
experts.

Other cases are more circumstantially oriented and show mild-
er symptoms. This can range from basic discouragement to more
complicated depression. When an aging parent is emotionally
down most of the time, the equilibrium of the care-givers can be
adversely impacted. It is challenging to spend large amounts of
time with persons who constantly complain about how awful everything is in life.

Once again the Word of God gives us instruction. In 1
Thessalonians 5:11 Paul writes, "Therefore encourage one another and build up one another, just as you also are doing." A few verses later he adds, "[14] We urge you, brethren, admonish the unruly,
encourage the fainthearted, help the weak, be patient with everyone." Everyone needs encouragement – especially those who are
"fainthearted" and "weak." It is our duty to compassionately help
them in their needs. With patience and persistence we should

encourage and build up those around us. Rather than ignoring the discouraged parent, or responding in kind, we should maintain a cheerful attitude of godly edification. Reminding them of God's past faithfulness, of His present goodness, and of the promises He has made of future blessing, we can direct their minds to the Lord.

Often the problem with disheartened people is that their attention is on the wrong person. They are looking at themselves rather than looking to the Lord. As long as they focus upon self, they grow more and more discouraged. When they lift their eyes to Him who made heaven and earth, it can quickly change their perspective for the better. Reading such passages as Psalm 121 will do no harm, and may do enormous good to those battling discouragement. Encouraging them to meditate on God's word can fill the void of discouragement with spiritual joy.

Questions for Discussion

- What is the stark reality about our parents that we must face? What experiences have you had with a difficult family member?
- What aspects of the fifth commandment are most challenging to you?
- According to Paul, how should we respond to evil? What should we not do? What should we do instead?
- What does Jesus require of us in Matthew 10?
- What does Hebrews 3:12-13 say to the Christian with an unbelieving parent?
- What is bitterness and what does it produce? How should a Christian respond to an embittered elderly person?
- How does the gospel resolve the problem of alienation?
- What can we do to counteract complaining, discouragement and mild depression?

CHAPTER 10

LOSS OF INDEPENDENCE

John 21:[18] "Truly, truly, I say to you, when you were younger, you used to gird yourself and walk wherever you wished; but when you grow old, you will stretch out your hands and someone else will gird you, and bring you where you do not wish to *go*." [19] Now this He said, signifying by what kind of death he would glorify God. And when He had spoken this, He said to him, "Follow Me!"

There are truisms in life – facts that are so obvious and self-evident, it is almost unnecessary to mention. These are realities beyond debate by reasonable people. One of these truisms is that we are all aging. This means that we are hastening to the day of our death. Although none of us knows the day of our death, we do not doubt that it is approaching and cannot be delayed.

The author of Ecclesiastes reflects on this when he says in Ecclesiastes 8:8 "No man has authority to restrain the wind with the wind, or authority over the day of death; and there is no discharge in the time of war, and evil will not deliver those who practice it." Even more to the point is Ecclesiastes 9:12 "Moreover, man does not know his time: like fish caught in a treacherous net and birds trapped in a snare, so the sons of men are ensnared at an evil time when it suddenly falls on them."

With aging come certain limitations. We experience restrictions and declining capacities physically, mentally and emotionally. We can no longer produce at the level we once achieved with relative ease. Our brains are not as absorbent and memory falters more frequently. Learning new information stretches our intellects to the breaking point. Emotionally speaking, we see ourselves being more fragile and brittle. Our ability to maintain our equilibrium is diminished, and we react badly at times.

A truism near and dear to Americans is their love of independence. American culture everywhere presupposes individuality and a freedom to "do my own thing." To be independent is to be alive – it is one of the cultural virtues revered as an "inalienable right." But as we age, we gradually lose our ability to maintain the veneer of independence.

To our amazement, we find ourselves increasingly dependent on those around us. We are forced to rely on the younger generation to do for us what we once proudly did for ourselves. As independence evaporates, and dependence grows, it creates challenges for everyone involved – the adult child and the aging parent. This loss tears at the fabric of our lives, and undermines societal values. We lose something important to our sense of self-worth, but there is little we can do to reverse the trend.

As the Lord Jesus told Peter, "When you grow old, you will stretch out your hands and someone else will gird you, and bring you where you do not wish to go." For Peter, that statement foreshadowed his death by crucifixion at the hands of the Roman Empire. Though most of us will never experience such an excruciating situation, the fact remains – we will lose our independence and others will lead, guide, dress and feed us.

What does that loss of independence involve? What are the challenges along the way? It often begins with the reduction of basic life skills. The interest in and ability to accomplish these tasks leads to frustration and conflict. These can involve cooking, eating, dressing, laundry, cleaning and housework, transportation, personal hygiene, medical care, financial management and more.

Along with the gradual decline, there are sometimes major turning points. When I was a boy I recall when my parents came to the conclusion that my Grandma could no longer drive safely. She had caused a traffic accident by basic inattention, and that triggered a discussion about her safety behind the wheel. Although the incident had not resulted in injury or death, it alerted her children that it was time to take the keys away and sell the car. Now she would need to be driven to church, the grocery store, the beauty shop, doctor's appointments and countless other places. For many seniors, this is one of the hardest parts of growing older. Other turning points can include the inability to maintain a house, condo or apartment, an incapability to live alone safely, or the loss of important relationships.

It is not uncommon that these major turning points become battle grounds between elderly parents and their adult children. Having always been "in charge," the parents struggle to accept the sensible advice of their children. Giving up the keys, accepting outside caregivers, moving from 'home' to assisted living or a nursing home, are all disputable points.

So what is the impact on the parents? How should they respond to the inevitable process of aging, and the loss of independence? One significant challenge is to "age graciously." This includes accepting God's wise and holy providence, and submitting to His will without arguing or complaining. This is not easily done, nor is it commonly seen. This response requires a level of spiritual maturity and theological awareness that not every senior has attained in earlier life.

Another challenge to elderly folks is to cope with temporal disappointments. An older friend of mine loved to eat, and steak was his favorite meal. Yet as he aged he could no longer chew or digest steak. His caregivers tried to give him steak pureed in a blender, but that was not the same. He had to give up something he had always enjoyed because his body could no longer handle it.

Dealing with caregivers – whether that be family members, medical personnel, or employees of a facility – is also sometimes difficult. When a caregiver asks an elderly patient to do something (or not do something), a decision is demanded. Will the patient cooperate or resist? Will they be compliant, or will they possibly become violent? What does an older person do if they are sometimes neglected by their caregivers? What should happen if the caregiver is rude, insulting or abusive? These dynamics can produce anger, despair or deep discouragement on the part of an elderly parent.

One of the biggest challenges for an elderly parent is knowing how to respond to one of the battle-ground issues with a child. When an adult child says, "Dad, I need your keys because it is no longer safe for you to drive," what will that parent do? Will he accept the advice and yield to his child? While it is undoubtedly difficult for a child to have such a conversation, it is even more challenging for a parent to face reality.

For all of us, recognizing our own mortality is an enormous challenge. We are reminded of this in Hebrews 9:27 "And inasmuch as it is appointed for men to die once and after this *comes* judgment," God has appointed a day when each of his creatures will die. When men and women die, they face the certain judgment of God. Most of the human race has expended enormous energy in suppressing this truth in unrighteousness. We are told in a thousand ways that we will live forever, even as we drive past cemeteries that remind us of the inevitability of death. God has placed eternity in our hearts, and we know instinctively that there is something beyond the grave. Will it be eternal life, or will it be the endless torment of hell, where the worm never dies and the fire never is extinguished? The older man grows, the more eternity looms before his sight. Though he may shut his eyes to that fact, he cannot escape the sense of the inevitable. This is perhaps the chief stress on an aging parent.

From the other side of the relationship, there are different stresses. The impact on adult children is no less acute. It begins with watching an "ageless" parent visibly and obviously aging. Growing up, I always looked to my dad as a pillar of strength and vitality. He remains remarkably vigorous in his 80th year of life, but I can tell he is aging. He readily admits that he tires more easily now.

Moses described this well in Psalm 90:9-10 "For all our days have declined in Your fury; We have finished our years like a sigh. [10] As for the days of our life, they contain seventy years, Or if due to strength, eighty years, Yet their pride is *but* labor and sorrow; For soon it is gone and we fly away." Watching that parental decline is painful for any child.

Another challenge for adult children is making unpopular decisions that will further limit the independence of the parent. When my parents and their siblings concluded that they could not allow my grandmother to drive, that was heart-wrenching for all of them. To tell her that she was not a safe driver anymore was even more difficult. A good portion of this difficulty is because roles have changed. The parent is now being treated like a child, while the child is acting in the role of parent. Mentally reconciling oneself with those role reversals is stressful on a child.

Then there is also the constant difficulties of providing care for dependent parents. It is not uncommon that adult children find themselves sandwiched between two needy groups. There are the dependent parents on one side, and their own children on the other side. Without neglecting needy parents, the adult child must continue to care for his own offspring. There are not enough hours in the day to give adequate time to both dependent parents and dependent children.

One the emotional level, adult children can be drained by the challenge of watching parents decline. Seeing the natural sadness of a mother or father as they lose their independence, the adult child goes through a grieving process also. When there are medical emergencies, the emotional rollercoaster can be intense. After a long day of caring for a needy parent and responding to all of the other demands of life, the adult child can be left emotionally exhausted.

The other side of this same coin is the time drain. To take an aging parent to a doctor's appointment can consume well over half the day. Driving to and from the appointment adds to the time commitment, and then there is a prescription to pick up at the pharmacy. Before anyone knows it, the entire day is gone with nothing else accomplished. The demand on time is an extreme stress for the adult child providing care for the parent.

In addition to the necessary commitments to the elderly parent, the adult child often has duties to their spouse, their children, their grandchildren, their church, their job, and their circle of friends. Juggling these many different responsibilities is challenging and requires a clear set of priorities.

Given a seemingly impossible task of keeping everyone happy, how does the Christian handle this situation? Let me suggest five ideas to help with coping:

1) Through conscious dependence upon Christ. "I can do all things through Christ, who gives me strength" Paul says. Such a complex load of responsibility can only be successfully handled through the strength that Christ provides.
2) Through a regular use of the 'means of grace.' Regular Bible reading and prayer are crucial for spiritual, mental, emotional and relational balance. Maintaining these spiritual disciplines are needful for all of life – and especially for these circumstances.
3) Through a faithful network of supportive believers in a sound church. Paul tells us to "bear one another's burdens,

and so fulfill the law of Christ." Churches should provide the burden-bearing support that Christ commands! This requires the church to be the church, and to help those who are particularly burdened.

4) Through maintaining healthy relationships with immediate family. To care for an aging parent, you need to love of your spouse and children. Though the immediate family sometimes gets pushed to the side, they are vital for maintaining balance. Furthermore, they should be part of the team of helpers discussed earlier.

5) Through a deepening love to and confidence in God. He is the one who has providentially assigned these circumstances, and has called you to "pay back" to your parents the love and care they gave to you in your young life. Thank God for giving you aging parents, and the ability to help them through the difficult days of old age.

Questions for Discussion

- What limitations come with inevitable aging? How do you see this in your own life, and the lives of those around you?
- What happens when people begin losing their independence? How do people tend to react to that loss?
- What are some significant turning points? What are battleground issues, and how should they be handled?
- What challenges do aging parents face during this decline? Can you think of other challenges than those mention in the chapter?
- What stresses do adult children face as they care for declining parents?
- What are the five strategies for coping with these difficulties? Which of these is most helpful to you now? Which of these should you develop in your life?

CHAPTER 11

MEDICAL ETHICAL DECISION MAKING

As medical knowledge, treatment and technology has advanced, a new set of concerns have been spawned that are "bioethical" in nature. Questions such as this intrude uninvited into our lives: "If we can medically sustain my terminally ill Grandma's life for another 6 weeks, should we?" How do we even begin addressing such quandaries? What guides us as we make the necessary "judgment calls" for aging relatives? Which motives are legitimate, which are illegitimate, and how do we differentiate between them?

"Ethics" can be generally defined as "the science of moral philosophy which teaches men their duty and the reasons for it" or "a system of moral principles." "Medical Ethics" are the subset of moral imperatives dealing with principles and duties touching the medical care of our physical bodies. Examples might include the use or removal of feeding tubes, the application of life-sustaining measures for comatose persons, or the wisdom of chemo-therapy for a frail parent in their late eighties.

Medical ethical issues have changed dramatically in recent decades, as Jesse Zeigler notes in <u>Medical Ethics, Human Choices</u>: "We face totally different questions in relation to medical care than did our parents and grandparents. For the most part this change has come about because of changes in technology that now make it possible to prolong life significantly and, thereby the process of dying. Increased life expectancy is a result, but the quality and meaning of that life have not always kept pace with the additional years." (Jesse H. Zeigler, "Ch. 7 Prolonging Life, Prolonging Death" <u>Medical Ethics, Human Choices </u>John Rogers, Editor; Herald Press, Scottsdale, PA, 1988; p.84)

David VanDrunen makes a further observation when he writes, "The experience of death and dying is a constant of all human history, and thus many of the moral issues that it provokes are perennial. But the explosion of biomedical technology in recent generations has altered the landscape at the end of life in countless ways. Many previously untreatable diseases are now curable, the lives of many terminally ill patients can be significantly prolonged, and the pain produced by fatal diseases can be minimized. (VanDrunen, David. <u>Bioethics and the Christian Life: A Guide to Making Difficult Decisions</u>; p. 169. Crossway. Kindle Edition.)

Within the realities of everyday life, not every bioethical case is black-and-white, right-and-wrong. Sometimes there can be two or more "rights", and not infrequently all the options appear to have some shade of "wrong" about them – the lesser of two evils. Willard S. Krabill writes "We should also define what we mean by *ethical dilemmas* in relation to medical-health care. A dilemma is a situation requiring a choice between at least two alternatives that are equally compelling and for which we can make equally strong cases. Modern medical technology has created many situations in which there is no simple right or wrong answer." (Willard S. Krabill, chapter 1 "Medical Ethics: Facing Difficult Questions;"

from <u>Medical Ethics, Human Choices</u> John Rogers, Editor; Herald Press, Scottsdale, PA, 1988; p.22.)

When thinking about aging parents and their medical conditions, any number of ethical problems can arise. As their conditions and capacities decline, who should make the decisions? Obviously the patient should be consulted about his or her wishes. The doctors and other medical professionals also have a say in the treatments contemplated. Of necessity, one or more children will typically participate in consultations. But what about the insurance company? Should it participate in treatment decisions, since it has a financial stake in the situation? Closely connected is the question of involvement by the civil government. If an elderly person's health care coverage is managed by a government agency (e.g. Medicare or Medicaid), then the voice of the civil authorities will be heard. Who has the "final say?" If the aging parent is incapable of making a decision, and there is no pre-existing determination (such as a "living will" or "power of attorney for health care"), who makes the hard call?

Another issue is the communication of information. When a parent has a serious medical condition, how much should they be told? Is it appropriate to withhold some of the information from them, or must we always tell "the whole truth?" If their mental ability to understand and process such information is restricted, should we try to tell them anyway? And a sticky question that frequently arises, "Is it ever permissible to lie to a parent?" If the parent suffers from dementia and can only be calmed by hearing certain false information, is it appropriate to communicate that admittedly incorrect information? What does it mean for an adult child to "speak the truth in love" to an ailing parent?

As death obviously approaches, the ethical issues intensify. Are we required to submit to treatment that sustains life, simply because it is available? Is it ever right to refuse treatment, if that means that death is hastened? What about suicide? Physician-assisted suicide? Euthanasia? These are "hot topics" in society today, and the culture rushes headlong toward euthanasia and doctor-assisted suicide without any moral qualms. But as Christians, our perspective is definitely different. Gilbert Meilaender aims for a balanced Christian position when he writes, "on the one hand, we ought not choose death or aim at death. But on the other hand, neither should we act as if continued life were the only, or even the highest, good. It is not a god, but a gift of God. Thus, we should neither aim at death nor continue the struggle against it when the time has come. "Allowing to die" is permitted. Killing is not. Within these limits lies the sphere of our freedom." (Gilbert Meilaender, Bioethics: a Primer for Christians. P.66 Grand Rapids: Eerdmans 2005.)

Meilaender goes on to note that some treatment options are essentially useless, and can be rejected without moral reservations. Other treatments can be useful, but unduly burdensome. He says, "Treatments that are useful and perhaps even lifesaving may some-times be excessively burdensome. Because life is not our god, we need not accept all burdens – no matter how great – in order to stay alive. We need to recognize clearly what this means. It means that we might rightly refuse even useful treatment that would pro-long our life for a significant period of time if that treatment re-ally does carry with it significant burdens. To reject or withdraw treatment because of its burdens is still a refusal of treatment, not of life." (Meilaender, Bioethics; p. 70.)

One component of such decision making is almost universal-ly ignored, and that is the financial aspect. If treatment is avail-able to sustain life temporarily, but is exorbitantly expensive, is it proper to consider financial issues in decision making? Can he-roic measures be rejected for financial reasons? Especially when a spouse and children will survive, is it good stewardship to press forward with costly care? Speaking personally, I would be very reluctant to leave my family hopelessly indebted for expensive medical treatments I received as part of a terminal illness. Do I have a moral right to refuse treatment that I deem unnecessarily expensive and injurious to my family's long term well-being?

So what are some biblical/theological principles that can help adult children and their aging parents navigate these medical ethical quandaries? First, we should embrace a full-orbed theology of life and death as found throughout the Scriptures. Human beings are created by the Sovereign God, and given meaning, purpose and significance. Our physical bodies are good in God's sight, and should be treated with dignity and respect. We reject Greek philosophical dualism that posits the physical body is evil and the immaterial spirit is good. Both body and spirit are created by God and have inherent worth. We are made in God's image, and that instills meaning into our physical existence. Though sin has marred that image, it is not entirely effaced.

These commitments also recognize that God is the author of life, that the Spirit is the Lord and Giver of life, and that Christ desires that we enjoy life "to the full." On the contrary, death is the great enemy of God and His people. Death is God's judicial punishment on Adam's sin, and is not morally neutral (as so many today popularly suppose). God intended life, and death is the necessary antithesis of that life. All medical ethical decisions should be made from that explicitly Christian worldview.

Another helpful Biblical theme is the doctrine of providence as it relates specifically to suffering. God has foreordained whatsoever comes to pass, and that often includes assignments of suffering for His children. Nothing in this life happens by chance apart from God's ordained approval. Job expressed this pointedly to his wife when she counseled him to abandon his integrity, curse God and die. He said to her in Job 2:10 "You speak as one of the foolish women speaks. Shall we indeed accept good from God and not accept adversity?" Positively, Christians should meditate upon the deep implications of Paul's words in Romans 8:28 "And we know that God causes all things to work together for good to those who love God, to those who are called according to *His* purpose."

As already noted in chapter 7, there is a complex of Biblical ideas relating to the connection between sin and sickness. Keeping those principles in tension can aid the decision making process.

In addition, we are reminded in James 1:5 "But if any of you lacks wisdom, let him ask of God, who gives to all generously and without reproach, and it will be given to him." This God-given wisdom is mediated by the Holy Spirit – that other Helper sent by Christ – the Spirit of truth. The Spirit is pleased to use the sacred Scriptures as a light to our path. Especially we should heed His commands. We are told in Psalm 119:98-100 "Your commandments make me wiser than my enemies, For they are ever mine. [99] I have more insight than all my teachers, For Your testimonies are my meditation. [100] I understand more than the aged, Because I have observed Your precepts." This divine wisdom is reinforced by godly advisors who can point us to the truths of God's word. This point is made in Proverbs 15:22 "Without consultation, plans are frustrated, But with many counselors they succeed."

A final point should be made that is by no means insignificant – all medical ethical issues should be the occasion for much prayer. When our Savior had decisions to make concerning his ministry, he resorted to prayer. In Luke 6 He determined to set apart certain disciples as apostles. These men would carry on the work of the church after His return to heaven – it was an important decision. What do we read? Luke 6:12 "It was at this time that He went off to the mountain to pray, and He spent the whole night in prayer to God. [13] And when day came, He called His disciples to Him and chose twelve of them, whom He also named as apostles."

Alone on a mountain, for an entire night he communed with His Heavenly Father in prayer. Beseeching His God, he wrestled and struggled to prayerfully make the correct appointments. We might suppose that if ever anyone could make important decisions without extended prayer, it was our Lord Jesus. Being fully and truly God, He could have made a perfect snap-decision. Yet He chose to pray prior to that decision.

Being fallible and finite human beings, we face many situations where we simply do not know what to do. Which way should we go? Seeking God in prayer prior to making such decisions is never a waste of time. Indeed, it is the best use of time. Why do we pray so little? Why do we make life-changing decisions without ever consulting the Lord? Too often we behave like foolish King Asa. In 2 Chronicles 16:12 we discover this sad footnote to his reign. "[12] In the thirty-ninth year of his reign Asa became diseased in his feet. His disease was severe, yet even in his disease he did not seek the LORD, but the physicians." How much wiser to have sought the Lord in prayer!

Questions for Discussion

- What are "ethics"? What are "medical ethics?" For the Christian, what is the standard of all our ethics?
- How have relatively recent medical advances changed the playing field?
- What do you think of Krabill's statement that "Modern medical technology has created many situations in which there is no simple right or wrong answer."
- Who should be involved in making medical ethical decisions? Why?
- Should an adult child ever lie to his or her aging parent?
- Is it ever right to refuse treatment? Under what circumstances could that be contemplated?
- What might be included in "a full-orbed theology of life and death as found throughout the Scriptures?"
- As Christians, what should we do prior to making an important medical decision for an aging parent?

CHAPTER 12

THE SPIRITUAL DIMENSION

In His infinite wisdom, God has designed an institution to care for the souls of His children, and that institution is the church. This covenant community is made up of people from all ages, places and backgrounds. It is the normal and natural experience for believers in Christ to be involved in the life of a faithful, Bible-believing and Bible-teaching church. Through this holy institution, God equips his people for service and enables them to do the work of ministry. It is within the church that young believers grow to full maturity. Here they are taught the doctrines of our most holy faith, and here they learn their various duties as followers of the Savior. In the worship of the church Christians can love the Lord their God with heart, soul, strength and mind, and also love their neighbors as themselves. Strong bonds of fellowship and communion develop as the church lives out its corporate life. As a result of the church, families are blessed, individuals are benefitted, and even society as a whole is enriched.

For the orderly care of his flock, God appointed under-shepherds. They are charged to keep watch over the spiritual welfare of the members. They must feed the sheep on the rich fare of God's word. They must comfort and encourage the weak and needy. These shepherds show their metal by defending the sheep from the wolves who would devour. Going out on the hills, they seek the wanderers in order to bring them back to the fold. When disease or injury besets the sheep, the shepherds bind up their wounds and nurse them back to health. One day those under-shepherds will give an account to the Great Shepherd of the sheep, even Jesus Christ.

When elderly members remain involved in the life of their church, the blessings abound in multiple directions. First, it is a blessing to an elderly member to continue his or her participation in the body of Christ. By being under the means of grace, their spiritual growth continues. In the church they receive the grateful love and care of the congregation. Not only that, but they continue to be fruitful for God's kingdom. David puts it this way in Psalm 92:13-15 "Planted in the house of the LORD, They will flourish in the courts of our God. [14] They will still yield fruit in old age; They shall be full of sap and very green, [15] To declare that the LORD is upright; *He is* my rock, and there is no unrighteousness in Him."

Not only is their involvement in the church a blessing for them, but it greatly benefits the congregation. Such mature believers serve as role models for the younger and less spiritually mature. As these senior saints take seriously their responsibilities in such passages as Titus 2:1-5, the older men can disciple the younger men and the more mature ladies can encourage the younger women. The potent combination of a lifetime of spiritual growth together with their numerous life experiences can be a treasure house for the congregation. Seeing believers who for decades have run the race with perseverance can stimulate others to keep on when they're tired and tempted to quit.

It is also of benefit to the biological family of that older believer. As we've seen in earlier chapters, the biological family has a primary responsibility to care for aging parents and grandparents. Yet biological families have limitations and need help. This is where the church can step in and help. In one case in our congregation, a widow was increasingly frail and needy. Her son lived three hours away, and could not always be available due to work and family responsibilities. When a crisis would arise, it would take him a minimum of three hours to be on hand. Members of the congregation were able to assist the widow and supplement care when the son was unavailable. The son was profoundly grateful for the ways the congregation assisted his mother, especially in his absence.

While this is the ideal, it is not always the reality. Sometimes elderly members stop attending church and "disappear" from view. In many cases this is understandable and necessary. If an older member cannot get out for church due to failing health and diminished strength, that is legitimate. In other cases, the older member simply loses interest in continued involvement. These situations include those who could participate, but choose not to attend.

In either scenario, the loss is significant for everyone. The older member can suffer spiritually, the congregation loses out on the blessings coming from its veteran members, and the bulk of the care lands squarely on the biological family.

What are some of the hindrances to participation? During years of relative health and strength, believers are sometimes tempted to diminish their involvement for many reasons. Extensive travel during retirement can lead to a sense of detachment from the local congregation. Churches in colder climates of the US often see the migration of "snowbirds" in the late autumn. Mostly older believers – sometimes including ordained leaders – leave for three to six months in warmer climates. During their absence, the life of the church continues. People come and go, difficulties arise and are addressed, and normal change takes place. When the snowbirds return from the south, a time of re-adjustment is typically required. Older members can feel displaced and unneeded, and younger members can be unsettled as well.

Not unrelated is the "retirement mentality" that exists within our culture. According to societal expectations, when a person turns 65, they are "retired" from active service and no longer are expected to contribute. They are free to indulge themselves in any pursuit they choose. This mentality migrates into the church, and older Christians are sidelined in favor of younger members. Those who are over 65 are frequently viewed as disengaged from congregational service, even though some actively resist being "put out to pasture." Thus when these mature saints have the most to offer in terms of wisdom and experience, they are deemed unnecessary. Sometimes it is voluntary, though not always.

Changing congregational demographics can also impact the involvement of seasoned veterans. With the influx of young families with little children, older members can wonder whether they still belong. "What is happening to 'my church' and do I matter anymore?" they can ask. The sense that the church they served for so long has changed can lead older members to either switch churches or stop attending altogether.

Other times the changes in attendance patterns are the result of spiritual apathy and laziness. It is not without reason that the author of Hebrews says, "10:23 Let us hold fast the confession of our hope without wavering, for He who promised is faithful; [24] and let us consider how to stimulate one another to love and good deeds, [25] not forsaking our own assembling together, as is the habit of some, but encouraging *one another;* and all the more as you see the day drawing near."

In times of sickness, weakness and infirmity the situation can be vastly different. A older member stops attending and at first, no one notices. The pastor and elders may be aware that "we have not seen so-and-so for a few weeks now," but no inquiry is made. Some time later – perhaps a long while later – the news arrives that this person has been seriously ill for that whole time.

Other legitimate conditions can arise that prohibit continued involvement. The inability to drive a vehicle can hold some back. Others have potentially embarrassing physical conditions and are fearful of causing "a scene" at church. Sometime getting out is too tiring and no longer feasible for an elderly church member. Sitting on hard pews is not as easy in old age as when you were a child. When a spouse dies, the widow or widower may find it traumatic to go to church alone. There are many understandable reasons that older members drift away from the life of the church.

How can the church facilitate involvement for older members? It begins with gentle encouragements to those who can still attend services and times of fellowship. Openly appreciating their participation and giving them realistic opportunities to serve can help them feel that they still belong to the body.

When resistance or reluctance is encountered, then gracious appeals serve better than stiff rebukes or caustic comments. Again, the Apostle Paul's words are instructive: 1 Timothy 5:1 "Do not sharply rebuke an older man, but *rather* appeal to *him* as a father, *to* the younger men as brothers, [2] the older women as mothers, *and* the younger women as sisters, in all purity."

Another strategy is to continuing using the gifts and abilities of these experienced servants of God, and to strongly resist any kind of "retirement" from service. Telling a Sunday School teacher that she may no longer teach the class she's led for the past thirty years is hurtful and counter-productive. Even when a change of this sort is necessary, it should be handled with supreme gentleness and kindness.

One of the better ways to keep the elderly members engaged is to specifically look for opportunities to integrate age groups and encourage the younger and the older to get to know one another. We have done this with our six children, and they have each had an older friend at church during their childhood. This has been enormously helpful to our children. Having that mature friend has pulled them up to a level of maturity not previously seen. It has also been enjoyable for the older men and women who participated in these relationships. In one case, an eighty year old man befriended my ten year old son. The relationship was as beneficial for our friend Charles as it was for my son Ian. They had a long lasting and sweet friendship that was mutually enjoyable and encouraging.

Lastly, when the day comes that elderly members can no longer attend services, it becomes the duty of the pastor, the elders, the deacons and even the members to reach out to the shut-in. Sometimes that means providing a meal or stopping by for a visit. Reading Scripture and praying with the older member is always appropriate. Phone calls and cards can also be great encouragements. The tendency is to forget those who no longer attend services. Out-of-sight, out-of-mind is too easy to practice. But we should not forget those who have been faithful members in the past, and who can no longer do what they once did. Diaconal ministry of this sort can be very rewarding,

Questions for Discussion

- What are the blessings of continued involvement for the older member? The congregation? The biological family?
- Why is non-involvement dangerous to all?
- What are some reasons that older saints stop attending church? Can you think of other reasons?
- What is the difference between legitimate and illegitimate reasons for non-attendance?
- How does the retirement mentality in American culture impact the church?
- What are some ways we can encourage older members to continue participating? Have you seen situations like this in your church?
- What should we do when an older saint can no longer attend? What are some ways to keep encouraging them spiritually?

CHAPTER 13

ASSISTED LIVING, NURSING HOMES, AND HOSPITALIZATION

Throughout this book we've been reflecting on the implications of the fifth commandment for adult children toward their aging parents. Of particular usefulness is the 127th question and answer of the Westminster Larger Catechism. The question is *"What is the honor that inferiors owe to their superiors?"* With typical Puritan thoroughness, the Westminster Divines give seven distinct aspects of honor. The fifth of the seven reads as follows: "fidelity to, defense, and maintenance of their persons and authority, according to their several ranks, and the nature of their places;"

Applying this to our topic, that answer suggests that adult children should demonstrate fidelity to their parents, should defend their parents, and must maintain their persons. This speaks of a proper loyalty to the parent as a parent. This is appropriate, since God has given that parent to that child, and vice versa. Familial loyalty, though rare in our modern world, is still a virtue to be celebrated. When the parent is vulnerable, the child should come to the defense of the parent. Protecting an elderly parent against those who would abuse or victimize them is simply part of being a good child. As the child sees the parent declining, and in need of maintenance, the child should be the very first to come to their aid. Allowing a parent to languish is sinful neglect, and cannot be countenanced.

These applications of the fifth commandment are seen clearly in Paul's first letter to Timothy, which we considered back in chapters 4 and 5. Especially in I Timothy 5, he focuses upon these duties. Consider again the following verses from that chapter: 1 Timothy 5:4 "but if any widow has children or grandchildren, they must first learn to practice piety in regard to their own family and to make some return to their parents; for this is acceptable in the sight of God...[8] But if anyone does not provide for his own, and especially for those of his household, he has denied the faith and is worse than an unbeliever... [16] If any woman who is a believer has *dependent* widows, she must assist them and the church must not be burdened, so that it may assist those who are widows indeed."

In this chapter Paul is dealing with various relationships within the church. He particularly focuses on widows and their care. In v.4 he suggests that children and grandchildren have a primary duty to practice piety toward widows within their own biological family, and can thus make some return to their parents. God approves of such filial fidelity.

In verse 8 he goes on to insist that Christians must provide for their own, especially for those within their own household. This is such a self-evident requirement that even unbelievers commonly do such. To neglect the proper maintenance of an aging parent is monstrous and constitutes a denial of the faith. It places the negligent Christian in a position of inferiority to the average unbeliever.

The practical side of this situation is highlighted then in verse 16. The church has many widows to assist, and limited resources simply will not allow for the financial upkeep of every needy case. Families must support their dependent widows so that the church can focus its attention on those who are "widows indeed" – those widows without families to assist them. So fidelity to, defense of and maintenance of their persons is a Biblical duty assigned to adult children toward their aging parents.

As parents age, their needs change and new challenges arise. Perhaps they can no longer negotiate the layout of their home without assistance. Climbing stairs can become a dangerous adventure. Walking on tile floors can result in painful falls. Bodily balance is not what it used to be, and a walker becomes a necessity. Simple tasks like taking the garbage to the street or walking the dog are exhausting at best, and become increasingly impractical.

Adult children can see their parent declining, and wonder whether the situation has reached a point where intervention is needed. Can Mom or Dad be left alone anymore? Does someone need to be on hand for bathing, dressing, mealtimes, and evening routines? When questions are posed, the elderly parent might be agreeable, may be in denial, or can prove somewhat hostile to the well-intended offers of help. Perhaps other family members or friends express similar concerns together with the urgent request, "Can't you do something about this?" There is no one-size-fits-all standard for when and how intervention takes place, though adult children can usually tell when "it's time." These decisions are judgment calls, and require courage, grace and wisdom. They are rarely easy for either side of the discussion.

So what should an adult child do when he or she has determined that help is needed? Where should they turn? One option is to open their own home to the aging parent, and welcome them into the family. That means the extended family become primary caregivers. This approach is approved by Scripture and has significant benefits. Having an aging parent living with you is one way to provide for them, assist them, and practice piety toward them. In the ancient world, this would have been the most common solution to challenges posed by parents in declining health. In many cultures around the world, this is still assumed to be the way such things are handled. Multiple generations living under one roof is not as foreign to other cultures as it is to American society.

That is not to say that this approach is easy, or that everyone can take an elderly person into their domicile. Sometimes the layout of the home is not conducive to care for an enfeebled person. There can also be space issues, such as the lack of an extra bedroom for the parent. If everyone in the household is gone during the day, having an elderly parent remain at home alone may scuttle the plan. Pre-existing intra-family hostilities can also make such an arrangement untenable for a long-term solution. When medical issues have arisen, the need for skilled care might require more than the family can provide or afford. In the case study of Lynn and Sandy in chapter 8, the monthly cost of around-the-clock in-home licensed caregivers was $20,000 in 2006. Their efforts to provide some of that care themselves proved too draining for these ambitious sisters, and that experiment was quickly abandoned. As these ladies have candidly told me, "This approach is not for everyone."

If having the aged parent live with the adult child proves impossible, then what other options exist? For many people an institution will be the obvious choice. In certain cases assisted living is the best option. This allows for semi-independence for a senior who can still do many things for himself or herself. This provides a sense of self-worth that can keep spirits high. There is also a sense of community and social interaction that exists within assisted living facilities. Common areas in these facilities allow for conversation, game playing, crafting and other activities that brighten life for an aging senior.

Different levels of care can be accessed if capabilities decline, though every new aspect of care has a price tag. If the senior needs help with eating meals, that service can be provided for a cost. The base price is often significant, and additional services increase the bottom line price. Even when insurance covers some of the cost, the price can be shockingly high. A member of my own extended family has been in such a facility, and the bill for a semi-private room runs around $8000 per month. For a private room the cost would be $16000 a month. In a high-end facility in that same community, it is reported that a one-time entrance fee of $250,000 is charged, with additional monthly charges on top of that.

In discussions with an administrator of a large facility in my community, he explained the dilemma faced by many nursing homes and assisted living centers. Because federal programs like Medicaid pay comparatively little for the services given to their clients, the facilities face the likelihood of bankruptcy if they do not find other sources of income. A high priced assisted living center can generate revenue to offset the financial losses experienced by the connected nursing home, and thus keep the whole operation solvent. Therefore younger, healthier, and wealthier clients of the assisted living center pay somewhat inflated prices that maintain the nursing facility.

When a parent declines significantly and can no longer do much for himself or herself, the next stage is almost inevitably a nursing home. Sometimes there is simply no other choice, especially when skilled medical care is required. These facilities can be a significant help to a family who cannot care for the parent themselves in their own home.

Anyone who has spent time in such a facility knows the downsides. Often these homes are understaffed, and the turnover of nurses is high. Low wages can be viewed as necessary, but often lead to inferior care. In at least some facilities, the financial realities dictate hiring strategies. Staff who have received a minimum of training are less costly than a Registered Nurse. Having two nurses per floor is less expensive than having three, four or five. Patient neglect can be a chronic problem due to the limitations experienced by the staff. To fully staff a facility with highly trained and properly credentialed people would prove too expensive, and rates for services would be necessarily increased to meet the cost.

At times the care provided to the residents can be impersonal, rude or even abusive. When my own grandfather was in the later stages of his cancer, I called the facility to talk with him and to say "good-bye" to a man I respected and loved. I was horrified to over-hear the nurse talking to him before handing him the phone re-ceiver. I remember thinking, "Do you know who you're talking to? That's my Grandpa! Do not treat him like that!" But since I lived hundreds of miles away at the time, there was little I could do.

Sometimes the abuse in nursing homes can come from fellow residents. Nurses and staff simply cannot police everyone at every moment. When dementia patients are present in a facility, the abuse from fellow residents can become violent and even criminal. Assault, theft and rape are not unheard of in some cases.

Similar pros and cons exist when hospitalization becomes nec-essary. The experience can be very positive and helpful to the patient. When attentive care is given by qualified medical profes-sionals, healing and restoration is promoted. At the same time, there can be hospital cases where the patient is neglected, ignored and even misdiagnosed and mistreated. The financial pressures on nursing homes are felt in hospitals also, and understaffing is not uncommon. For decades the medical world has been follow-ing the business model of Pharaoh, king of Egypt. His basic ap-proach is summarized in Exodus 5:18 "So go now *and* work; for you will be given no straw, yet you must deliver the quota of bricks." Downsizing medical staff has not meant diminished expectations of output. The same amount of work is required of fewer staff, and has led to reduced quality of care. As a pastor, I see this every time I visit a church member who is in the hospital. I feel badly for both the staff and the patients, for the realities of modern medicine impacts both sides of the equation. The ubiquitous demand to "boost the bottom line" pinches everyone connected to the medical process.

What should Christian adult children do to care for their parents if and when they must enter a facility? The first suggestion is to view yourself as the defender and advocate of your parent. In fidelity to your mother or father, you must speak up for their care. Demanding excellence and rejecting mediocrity from the facility and the staff will directly impact your parent's quality of life. This necessarily requires that you do your homework on the facility that you choose. Visiting the facility and observing the residents is vital. Reading a brochure or scrolling through a website is simply not enough. Go there, look at what they do, ask direct questions and demand specific answers. If you choose a facility, do not stop watching, listening and observing. Ongoing research will be needful, especially as staff come and go. Watch how other residents are typically treated, because that is how your family member will likely be handled when you are not present.

Second, you must avoid "warehousing" your elderly family members. Visit as frequently as feasible, and spend significant time with them. They are still your parent, and you are still their primary caregiver, even if they are in a facility receiving care from medical staff. To shuttle them off to a facility and forget they exist is unconscionable. Even if this means major changes in your routines, you have a duty to love them as you love yourself.

Attend to their spiritual needs, in connection with your church leaders. Those who live in institutions continue to have the same spiritual needs they had before. They do not stop being Christians because they are now in a nursing home. They should be encouraged through the word of God and prayer. Opportunities for Christian fellowship can and should be provided. Pastors, elders and deacons should be encouraged to visit on occasion. Their ministry can support and enhance your efforts to strengthen the faith of your parent.

Finally, listen carefully to your parent. They are the one living in that facility, and they know what goes on around the clock. Giving due attention to their complaints and requests helps you to help them.

Questions for Discussion

- What does it mean to "demonstrate fidelity to, to defend and to maintain their person?"
- How does 1 Timothy 5 spell out this approach?
- What are some of the new challenges that arise for aging parents? Can you think of other challenges?
- What are the pros and cons of taking a parent into your home? Would this be feasible for you?
- What are the pros and cons of an assisted living center? Of a nursing home?
- What does it mean to be a defender and advocate for your parent? How do you feel about that task?
- What is meant by "warehousing" the elderly? How can it be avoided?
- How can you continue to meet the spiritual needs of your parent when they are in a facility? What would be some practical plans for this area of responsibility?

CHAPTER 14

THE FINANCIAL REALM

Years ago I had an experience which significantly impacted me. I was having lunch at a Cracker Barrel restaurant in Lansing, Michigan with some family members. When we entered the restaurant, it was moderately busy. Within a few minutes of being seated, the dining area suddenly filled up with senior citizens. We had seen a bus pull into the parking lot, but thought nothing about it. As these seniors conversed around their tables, we could overhear some of their discussion. It gradually dawned on me that they were all being driven to a nearby casino. The casino had sent a bus to pick them up and bring them in, like sheep to the slaughter. These elderly folk did not appear to be excessively wealthy, but they were happily anticipating their afternoon of gambling. Most of them probably did not have a lot of extra money, but the casino would probably end up with most of their cash by the end of that day.

It is said that predators prey on the weak and the elderly. Such people are the easiest targets not only for casinos, but for scam artists and con men the world over. Here is an area where elderly parents are particularly vulnerable to attack, and desperately need to be defended and protected by their adult children. Although I am not a financial counselor or an investment advisor by trade, I do know certain things to be true. Moreover, there are important financial realities of modern life that everyone needs to consider.

Let's begin by looking at some vital financial issues for seniors, and then consider some practical ways that adult children can assist their parents. Most basic might be the fact that money management can become too difficult for an elderly person. Whether this is paying monthly bills, balancing the checkbook, doing taxes or managing retirement assets, the tasks can become overwhelming. We all realize that when certain financial transactions are not made in a timely manner, consequences follow. If the electric bills sit on the counter unopened and unpaid, the power will be turned off sooner or later. If checkbooks are not occasionally balanced, accounts can be overdrawn and costly fees incurred. This is the entry level issue for the financial realm, and is probably the first need to be addressed. Something as simple as arranging automatic payments for recurring bills can ease the strain on aging seniors and their adult children.

Another common problem is when elderly people receive persuasive counsel from insurance agents, stockbrokers or other financial advisors who are pushing improper financial products. Such salesmen may be unethical, or may simply have good intentions, but offer a limited assortment of financial products. Although they may sincerely believe that their product is best for every senior, that is not always the case. Examples might include certain types of annuities and reverse mortgages. Aging parents and their adult children should carefully investigate financial products making promises which seem too good to be true. A simple internet search can turn up helpful information from law enforcement about financial scams commonly practiced upon the elderly.

Connected to this first issue is another problem that makes righteous hearts sick. I'm talking about financial abuse by family members of their own elderly relatives. In many states this is a felony. A son or a daughter is put on the checking account, and is given free access to all the financial resources of the parent. Perhaps at first it is a small amount here or there. When no one detects the transaction, the sinner grows bolder by degrees. Now larger amounts are being pilfered for personal purposes. Eventually accounts can be emptied and the child has stolen the parents' money. Such theft can also be carried out by caregivers and personal attendants.

Elderly parents who help out their adult children by lending them money can also become a potent source of trouble. This often begins when one child experiences an unexpected financial setback, such as a job loss or divorce. The parents typically see their assistance as honorable and necessary to stave off further problems (mortgage foreclosure, added marital strife, pulling grandchildren out of private school, etc.), even in cases where the child's financial crisis was clearly due to their own poor choices. Sadly, the child's need often persists and grows, consuming savings which the parents may well require for their own care late in life. Family strife may arise as siblings catch wind of the magnitude of mom and dad's "loans"; unless such amounts lent (and any repayments) are carefully documented, that strife will likely escalate later if all the children are expected to help cover the parents' nursing home bills. The proverbial final nail in the coffin will often be settlement of the parents' estate, as the lack of accurate records precludes a division of the inheritance assets in a way that all find fair. An angry "You received your share years ago!" and a fractured family may be the sad legacy of elderly parents who were only trying to help.

Another challenge for older adults is to plan properly for retirement, and then to strategically use those assets over their remaining years. This is where a trustworthy financial counselor or investment advisor can be invaluable. Because they specialize in these areas, they can give prudent help to their older clients.

If a convincing swindler comes along and suggests some outlandish scheme, the investment adviser can hopefully steer his clients clear of disastrous decisions. Even here, the child needs to remain alert, as their parents may make decisions without notifying their counselor.

There can also be an important role in this realm for other professionals, such as accountants and lawyers. Certain legal arrangements can have value in protecting an aging parent. By giving attention to account security for personal and financial information, the child can help organize the parent's affairs. Wills, trusts and powers of attorney can also play an important role. However, the main safeguard for an aging parent is an attentive child who will regularly interact openly with the parent, especially when the parent is hospitalized, becomes incompetent, or approaches death. If the parent will allow an adult child to think and talk through significant financial transactions before decisions are finalized, the parent can be protected from unscrupulous thieves.

It is ideal for older adults to have three advisers: a reputable attorney, an accountant, and a financial adviser. The financial adviser will likely have most regular contact with the senior, the accountant will be consulted less frequently, and the attorney as needed. There are significant benefits to involving an adult child in these conversations from time to time. Oral, and perhaps written permission might be necessary in order for the child to be privy to certain information. If unusual financial activity is noticed by the financial adviser, discussing the matter with an adult child can significantly help protect the parent.

In our society attorneys are typically viewed with skepticism. Jokes abound about greedy lawyers whose meddling only makes matters worse. Not infrequently people will download legal documents from the internet and fill in the blanks, thinking this is equivalent to the work of a good attorney. However, finding and using a reputable lawyer can be one of the more important decisions made for both aging parent and adult child.

One mistake that is sometimes made is to add a child as a signatory on a parent's bank account. If that account contains more than $26,000, there may be gift-tax implications, as the IRS may view the transaction as effectively making a gift of half the account's value to the child. Also, by adding the child as a joint account holder, the parent is now legally and financially linked to their child. For example, if a lawsuit were to be brought against the child, the parent's account would be vulnerable.

One of the unanticipated consequences of modern medical progress is that people are routinely living much longer. Meeting people in their nineties is not as uncommon today as in former generations. If they retired at the age of 65 that means that their resources will need to stretch over 35 years. If they have costly medical procedures done, or enter assisted living or a nursing home, their dwindling assets can be quickly depleted. Retirement facilities of all sorts routinely deal with residents who have outlived their retirement assets. What happens when all of mom and dad's money has been spent, and they have no more? Generous pension programs from past employment are increasingly rare, and free long-term health care for the retired is almost unknown. The expectation is that most retirees will end up on the government's rolls through Medicare and Medicaid. Yet the long-term viability of those government entitlements is also questionable. Understanding these programs and what they offer can be confusing to an elderly parent in failing health. Children can play a vital role in navigating these waters.

For adult children, financial crises of this sort could not come at a worse time. Although they are still in their prime wage earning years, there are other priorities demanding financial help. Children's college tuition is notorious for draining parental coffers. College graduates may find it difficult to obtain employment.

Increasingly these young adults are moving back in with their parents, and continue to be financially dependent. An epidemic of personal indebtedness also exacerbates the financial situation. In addition to helping elderly parents and paying college tuition, those adult children can find themselves floundering in credit card debt. So how much can they realistically contribute to helping their parents? This can cause serious stress, and lead to bitterness, harshness and other sinful responses.

Another subset of financial issues has to do with the estate of the parents. Due to a haphazard and unorganized approach, the settling of an estate after death can be a trying ordeal for the surviving family members. Due to a toxic combination of grief and greed, impatient children can wonder, "When are we getting our inheritance?" The more assets, and the greater the variety of assets, the longer the process typically lasts. In most cases, it is prudent to avoid probate at all costs. When the state becomes involved in distributing the assets, the wishes of the parents will be secondary to the expediency of the court.

Without careful pre-planning and wise directives from the deceased, the division of assets can spawn virtual fratricide. Envy and strife go hand in hand as the parental possessions are divided among children and grandchildren. Old rivalries can gain new life as one sibling covets what another receives, and vice versa.

So how should Christian adult children help their parents navigate the financial world? Here are five practical suggestions to consider:

1) Pay close attention to your aging parent's financial status and talk with them occasionally about their current situation. Gently asking questions can sometimes uncover areas where they struggle. Offers of help if and when needed can further assure them of your concern and willingness to assist.

2) Seek out and utilize trustworthy financial experts. If possible, be involved with the parent and his or her financial advisors. If the counselors know the child and understand the complementary role the child is playing, crises can be avoided or handled more effectively in the future. This also provides an extra set of eyes and ears for the elderly parent. If the parent does not understand what the financial adviser is suggesting, the child may be able to interpret for them. Adult children should make sure they clearly understand the costs and fees associated with financial products and advice, as wells as the risks, rewards, and potential for loss.

3) Centralize and simplify as much as possible. Having various accounts here, there, and everywhere can be confusing to everyone. Is there one place or person that serves as the headquarters for the parents' financial situation? One way to simplify is to have only a trustworthy biological child exercising responsibility for parental assets.

4) Maintain transparency and accountability. The temptation to steal is greater when there is little or no accountability. In order to avoid the depletion of assets, there should be checks and balances in place. Having an outside person occasionally audit the assets can serve as a deterrent to the unscrupulous.

5) Monitor your own attitudes about money. God's word warns us in 1 Timothy 6:10 that "The love of money is a root of all sorts of evil, and some by longing for it have wandered away from the faith and pierced themselves with many griefs." In Hebrews 13:5 on we are exhorted to "*Make sure that* your character is free from the love of money, being content with what you have; for He Himself has said, "I WILL NEVER DESERT YOU, NOR WILL I EVER FORSAKE YOU," Godliness with contentment is great gain, but the love of wealth can shipwreck the soul. When a child thinks about the assets accumulated by

a parent over a lifetime, the child should remember that this money is God's money first, secondarily it is the parent's money and only after that does it become the child's money.

Questions for Discussion

- What are some ways you've seen elderly folk victimized by unscrupulous people?
- What signs would indicate that an elderly parent can no longer effectively manage his finances?
- What professional expertise can children call upon for their aging parents? What role should the child play in these discussions?
- What is meant by "outliving one's retirement assets"?
- What other financial stresses can impact adult children trying to help their parents?
- What problems can arise with the estate after death? How can this be counteracted?
- Discuss the practical suggestions for helping aging parents with finances. Which is most challenging for you?

CHAPTER 15

HONORING PARENTS AT DEATH AND AFTERWARD

Funerals are emotional experiences for everyone involved, including the pastor who officiates the service. Having done more than my fair share of funerals, I can assure you that I'm almost always emotionally impacted one way or another. Sometimes funerals can be extremely encouraging, such as a funeral for the mother of a member of my congregation. During the service there was a time for remembrances of the deceased. Person after person recalled the many wonderful qualities of this lady, and how she had touched many lives for good. I left that funeral wishing I had known this amazing woman while she was yet alive.

Another funeral held a quite different experience. As the only son of the deceased stood up to eulogize his mother, he told a story that he must have thought to be funny. In the course of his anecdote, he revealed some of her shortcomings in the kitchen. The end result appeared to be ridiculing his mother and making her look hopelessly inept. He seemed to dishonor his mother and it left a sour taste in my mouth.

The fifth commandment continues to require us to honor our parents as they approach death, during their funeral service, and even afterwards. Proceeding chronologically, let's think first about these duties at the time of death. A Biblical model of loving care can be found in how Joseph honors his dying father Jacob. This example is well documented in Genesis 48-50 and is worthy of careful consideration.

What are some practical ways that an adult child can honor their parent as death approaches? It must being with providing care as the parent declines. Visiting them in the hospital, spending time at their bedside, overseeing their medical care and maintaining their comfort to the greatest degree possible. All of these are good ways to express affection.

Another way to honor them is to attempt to reconcile any past grievances while they are still able to converse. This can mean confessing wrong and asking for forgiveness, or it can include granting forgiveness. Both of these actions can be difficult, especially if the parent was in the wrong previously. When a parent will not admit their sin, or ask forgiveness, the problem can seem intractable. However, we can freely forgive others even if they do not specifically confess fault or ask for forgiveness. Letting go of bitterness is freeing for an adult child of a difficult parent. The other type of discussion can also contain challenges. To humbly admit to your parent that "I was wrong, please forgive me" takes courage. To do so without any rationalizations or justifications can be even more challenging. Yet there is nothing wrong with owning our sins and admitting them freely.

Still another duty to pursue while the parent is still coherent is the expression of appreciation. Every child has something to appreciate in a parent, even if it is only the fact that they biologically contributed to your birth. Taking the opportunity to say "Thank you for all you've done for me" can soften the callouses that build up over years.

Being with a parent when they die is a hard, but good thing. This is not always possible, especially if the parent and the child live in different regions of the country. Sometimes death is sudden and unexpected, and it is impossible to attend them at that moment. The scene at Jacob's death is touchingly recorded in Genesis 49:33-50:1 When Jacob finished charging his sons, he drew his feet into the bed and breathed his last, and was gathered to his people. [1] Then Joseph fell on his father's face, and wept over him and kissed him." With all of his sons surrounding him, the patriarch breathed his last and died. Immediately Joseph fell on his father's face, weeping and kissing his beloved parent.

Once the spirit has departed, it is important to care for the body of the parent. Though it is popularly denied by many grieving people, that body is still "my dad" or "my mom." True, their soul is no longer there. Yet Christianity does not teach that a person consists only of their soul or spirit. The body is part of the person, and that body will rise again at the final day. Again we look to Joseph's example in Genesis 50:2-3, "Joseph commanded his servants the physicians to embalm his father. So the physicians embalmed Israel. [3] Now forty days were required for it, for such is the period required for embalming. And the Egyptians wept for him seventy days."

At the time of death, it is important to care for the surviving family. An example can be gleaned from our Savior himself, albeit in a somewhat backward fashion. Fittingly, John records the scene in John 19:25-27 "But standing by the cross of Jesus were His mother, and His mother's sister, Mary the *wife* of Clopas, and Mary Magdalene. [26] When Jesus then saw His mother, and the disciple whom He loved standing nearby, He said to His mother, "Woman, behold, your son!" [27] Then He said to the disciple, "Behold, your mother!" From that hour the disciple took her into his own *household*."

Knowing that his own death was immanent, Jesus anticipated that his mother Mary would need care in future days. He especially loved and trusted one of his disciples – almost certainly John the Apostle. Thus he made a transfer, giving Mary to John and John to Mary. They were now to relate as a mother to a son, and vice versa. It is likely that John was Jesus' biological cousin, and therefore a member of his extended family. Jesus is thereby practicing what Paul would later advise in I Timothy 5 for family members to care for their own widows.

One last way to honor a parent in the time of their death is by constructing a fitting obituary to be published in local papers. Funeral homes often assist in this process and can craft a fitting tribute to the deceased. By highlighting their gifts and graces, while downplaying their weakness and failings, we publicly honor the parent to the community. Because of the long reach of the internet, this can touch the lives of people who may be unable to attend a visitation or a funeral service. As in all things, we want to speak the truth in love as we memorialize a family member who has passed from this life to the next.

Once the parent has passed away, there is frequently a blizzard of details, arrangements and responsibilities. God's good gift of adrenalin can enable adult children to handle a significant process in a period of a few days, particularly when other family members offer support, help and encouragement. Here is a sampling of questions to be faced: Which funeral home will be used? What arrangements have already been made, and what needs to be handled quickly? Will there be a visitation? When? Who will participate? How long should it last? Will there be a funeral service, or some sort of memorial service? When? Where? Who will officiate? What will be included in the service? Are there special songs, or favorite Bible passages to include? Will there be eulogies given? If so, by whom? Will there be a graveside committal? When and where? Will there be a meal after the graveside? Who will provide that, and where will it happen? Who is coming, where will they stay, and how long will they remain?

How do we pay for all of this? Is there insurance? Has anything been pre-paid?

If a visitation is held, and friends come to pay their last respects, this can be another way to honor the deceased parent. Frequently photographs are displayed from the person's life. This can be a good visual reminder and can highlight the good qualities of the person. There is also opportunity to converse with friends, family and members of the community about the parent. Taking time to extol their commendable traits and to voice appreciation will set a tone for others involved. An easy way to phrase this is to say, "One thing I always appreciated about my mom was ..." This can encourage others to recall things they appreciated. Although the visitation does often focus on the grief of the survivors, that is not the only purpose for such an event. Doing your fifth commandment duty at a visitation can instill a more positive and edifying tone to the time.

When the adult child is a believer, it is important to coordinate with the officiating minister. I've been on the receiving end of such discussions and they always help me to minister more effectively to the grieving family. One fact is very important to establish, if at all possible: the spiritual state of the deceased. If the parent was a professing Christian, that affords much comfort. If they were clearly a non-Christian and made no profession of faith in Christ, that is handled differently. If there are doubts or questions, the minister should know that also. It goes without saying that ministers should not lie, especially in the pulpit. To misrepresent the person as a Christian when they were not is wrong. "Preaching them into heaven" at the funeral will not save their lost souls. The truth must be told as clearly, charitably and lovingly as possible.

Often the most direct opportunity to honor a deceased parent comes during the time for eulogies in the service. Sometimes the surviving family is too overcome with grief to say anything publicly. But if an adult child can summon the composure to say "good words" to honor that parent, the fifth commandment is practiced to a listening audience. Recently I attended a funeral where an adult daughter spoke eloquently about her dead mother, and what a good and faithful woman she had been. I did not know either the daughter or the mother, but I found her eulogy to be very moving. I thanked her later for obeying the fifth commandment and publicly loving her mother.

In the area I live, the expectation is for a meal to be served to those who attend the funeral – typically after the graveside committal is done. Usually friends and family return to the church for a luncheon or light supper. Here is yet another opportunity to practice the fifth commandment. The adult child of a deceased parent will usually feel some relief and closure. The funeral service is over, the body is buried, and that chapter closes. But with so many sympathetic people around, it is possible to cheerfully remember the lost loved one.

Psychologists tell us that there are various "stages of grief" that most people experience. To a certain extent that is true, and we see that in those that mourn a death. Once the rush of the funeral week is past, guests have returned to their homes, and the adrenaline has stopped pumping through our bodies, we come to terms with the new reality. That mother or father, who has meant so much to me, is now gone. What next?

When physical and emotional equilibrium has returned, it is still good to honor our parents. Western culture does not venerate the dead, as happens in Asian countries. Yet we should not forget the dead either. The general scriptural pattern involves recollecting the events of past lives, and remembering them in an appropriate way. As Paul tells the Corinthians in 1 Corinthians 10:11 "Now these things happened to them as an example, and they were written for our instruction, upon whom the ends of the ages have come." Interestingly, Paul cites numerous negative examples from Israelite history. They serve as warnings to Christian believers.

In a positive vein, Hebrews 13:7 says, "Remember those who led you, who spoke the word of God to you; and considering the result of their conduct, imitate their faith." While this passage has special reference to apostles, ministers, elders and teachers, it can also apply more broadly to godly parents. When we were children, our parents provided leadership. If they were faithful, they probably read the Bible to us (cf 2 Timothy 1:5 and 3:15). We saw Christianity lived out in their lives as we matured. Now think back to their conduct, and the results of their faith. As you consider it, imitate their faith. The implication is that similar outcomes may result from your imitation of their conduct.

In conclusion of this study, let me encourage my readers with one last passage: In James 1:22-25 we read, "But prove yourselves doers of the word, and not merely hearers who delude themselves. [23] For if anyone is a hearer of the word and not a doer, he is like a man who looks at his natural face in a mirror; [24] for *once* he has looked at himself and gone away, he has immediately forgotten what kind of person he was. [25] But one who looks intently at the perfect law, the *law* of liberty, and abides by it, not having become a forgetful hearer but an effectual doer, this man will be blessed in what he does."

Having gone through this study and considered many important facets of the fifth commandment, it is now time to be "doers of the word." Having heard and discussed the word does not good if you do not follow it up with obedient action. If there is no change in commitments or conduct, the study has been in vain. If we do put into practice what we have heard as "effectual doers," God promises us that we will be blessed in what we do. Thus it is vital for us and our aging parents that we implement what God's word teaches. It will bring joyful blessings to our own lives, and to the lives of our parents in their later years. May God indeed bless you as you follow His word of truth!

Questions for Discussion

- What three time periods are identified in this chapter?
- How can an adult child honor their parent as the parent approaches death?
- How did Joseph honor Jacob at the time of his demise?
- What does Jesus teach about the care of surviving family members?
- How can the fifth commandment shape the time of visitation before the funeral?
- In what ways can an adult child positively contribute to the actual funeral service?
- How can children honor their deceased parents in the years following?

ABOUT THE AUTHOR

Brian L. De Jong is the minister of Grace Orthodox Presbyterian Church in Sheboygan, Wisconsin. He is married to DeLou, and they have six children.

De Jong realized the challenges of eldercare when his parents and mother-in-law started needing help. *Honoring the Elderly* is based on his own experiences and discussions in his Sunday school class.

Made in the USA
Monee, IL
13 September 2019